Praises for EFT Level 2 (Training Reso

This book constitutes a stunning example of professional mastery in this field – one which can be of help to any serious student of EFT whether or not they are taking formal Level 2 training. Ann Adams, a leader of EFT education worldwide, has teamed up with a major talent, EFT Trainer Karin Davidson, to clarify the advanced concepts of EFT and simplify them for us remarkably. Anyone interested in moving beyond the basics in EFT or who wants to learn to use it to help others, will love this book!

— Patricia Carrington, Ph.D., EFT Master – www.MasteringEFT.com

Here is the "state of the art" training in EFT. It is written by two of the most experienced and competent EFT practitioners. You owe it to yourself and your clients to make this book part of your library. It is a "MUST" read.

— Sandi Radomski ND, LCSW, Creator of Allergy Antidotes™, Co-creator of Ask & Receive™ – www.AskAndReceive.org

In today's world of stress uncertainty and fear-based living, Karin Davidson and Ann Adams are providing us with a divine opportunity to regain a sense of sanity, calm, and equilibrium. EFT Level 2 Comprehensive Training Resource is a clear, user friendly exploration of a self-help, self-healing technology that can and will put you back in the driver's seat in your life.

— Iyanla Vanzant, Spiritual Life Coach, EFT Level 3 Practitioner, Author, "In The Meantime" and "Peace from Broken Pieces"

Ann and Karin did a stellar job writing this manual. It is comprehensive in scope and easy to understand even for beginning tappers. This resource is a perfect adjunct for live trainings, as the content follows the Level 2 curriculum succinctly. This book should be in every EFT practitioner's library."

— Forrest Samnik, LCSW, EFT Trainer, Matrix Reimprinting Trainer, Hypnotherapist – www.LifeWorksWithEFT.com

Authoritative and extremely well written, this Level 2 companion volume to the EFT Comprehensive Training Resource Level 1 is outstanding. It would be easy for this information to be dry and difficult to read, but Adams and Davidson successfully avoid that mistake with

an organized, clear, easy to understand, and well-referenced guide. You'll advance your EFT training with confidence that the material presented is solid.

– Loretta Sparks, EFT Founding Master, DCEP, AAMET Trainer, TFTDX, Licensed Psychotherapist, Past President of the American Academy of Psychotherapist, Author – www.SelfCarePower.com

This is a fantastic and comprehensive resource for any serious therapy practitioner. It is much more than just a training manual on how to correctly use EFT to Level 2. It answers all the questions that any student may have in a live training but aren't answered due to time constraints. I, for one, will be recommending this to all my students whether studying EFT or not – the explanations on reframes, writings on the walls, and ethics are so important that they are universal for any serious practitioner.

– Richard Flook, Author of Why am I Sick? and META-Medicine Master Trainer – www.WhyAmISick.com

Ann Adams and Karin Davidson have written a well-designed and comprehensive EFT manual that you'll want to keep on your desk as an everyday reference. Whether you are an accomplished EFT'er or new to this amazing process, this book will educate, enlighten, and help you become more effective as a practitioner.

– Wendy Merron, BCH, CC-EFT – www.WendyMerron.com

I was an EFT Master and Trainer for years before I began to develop Matrix Reimprinting and this is one of the clearest and most comprehensive coursebooks on EFT concepts that I've seen. Even if you've begun to use new techniques from Energy Psychology, it's important to have a solid grounding in the original EFT concepts and techniques. I highly recommend reading this as a companion to any EFT training.

– Karl Dawson, Creator of Matrix Reimprinting, Hay House Author – www.MatrixReimprinting.com

The Level 2 EFT Resource is SO thorough and clear! All of the various alternatives and techniques are explained carefully. The examples and case studies are particularly helpful in understanding the application of the techniques. I highly recommend this book to those who are looking for a comprehensive, understandable guide to using EFT as a practitioner, or for their own deep use.

– Pamela Bruner, Business Success Coach, Author and EFT expert – www.MakeYourSuccessEasy.com

I just took a couple hours to read through the EFT Comprehensive Training Resource Level 2 and I was very impressed. To put it simply: This Level 2 Training Manual rocks! I've have been actively studying, practicing, using and teaching EFT to my coaching clients for many years. I have read and studied many EFT books and video materials. *I had recently read the related EFT Level I Resource (which I really liked), and I was happy to discover that the Level 2 Resource took the conversation into much deeper and richer territory. I have read many books on EFT and to date I have not run across anything quite as comprehensive and well put together as this book. It gives many clear examples and walks you through the many different aspects of working with clients. The chapters are powerfully user-friendly with summaries, tests, and exercises. And this book covers EFT from so many angles that it's now my go-to book to figure out how I might get EFT to work more effectively for myself and my clients. Thank you Karin and Ann for your contribution to the EFT world. I believe that many people will get hooked on sharing EFT and using EFT with others by reading this book.*

– Joseph S. Mitchell III, Esquire – www.ActivateYourGreatness.com

Attending workshops is a great way to learn EFT, but, when workshop attendees are busy learning new skills while working through their own issues, they can miss important concepts. This comprehensive manual is an invaluable resource for any serious student of EFT. The book is thorough enough to stand alone as a self-study guide, but it's *also the perfect companion to live trainings and workshops. If you're a student, get it for yourself. If you're a trainer, save yourself a lot of preparation work by providing it for your students.*

– Alina Frank, EFTU and Matrix Reimprinting trainer and mentor – www.JumpStartYourEFTPractice.com

I just finished the Level I coursebook and could not believe the enrichment I received from that one. And here is the Level 2 coursebook and it surpasses the first book! This book is beautifully illustrated and thoroughly supported with examples and insight that can only be gained through experience. Even though I have taken classes from both *Ann and Karin, the additional material and review is so powerful, it was like being in the classroom again, but in my pajamas with the capability of stretching the learning out as long as I wanted. Thanks for your usual high level of giving.*

– Lucy Shaw, ND, MBA and Author – www.HeartWorks4U.com

Kudos to Ann Adams and Karin Davidson for this excellent contribution to the EFT world. Their EFT Level 2 Coursebook is an invaluable comprehensive resource for students and teachers of EFT, and for all who are interested in this remarkable healing technique. Anyone who wants to understand and master essential EFT principles and art of delivery skills will want a copy of this book on their shelf, both to use and to share.

    – Betty Moore-Hafter, MA, CHT, AAMET Certified EFT Trainer, Co-Editor for EFTfree.net – www.CreativeEFT.com

This beautifully designed and extremely thorough EFT manual by Ann Adams and Karin Davidson teaches all of the advanced level material with the added bonus of more in depth and specific knowledge about EFT in theory and practice. The manual is very easy to follow even by lay people and will be an asset for all EFT trainers and students, during the certification training as well as an invaluable resource for years to come.

    – Ingrid Dinter, AAMET certified EFT trainer and coach – www.IngridDinter.com

EFT Level 2 Comprehensive Training Resource

Ann Adams and Karin Davidson

Energy Psychology Press
P.O. Box 442, Fulton, CA 95439
www.energypsychologypress.com
Cataloging-in-Publication Data

Cover design by Victoria Valentine
Copy editing by Stephanie Marohn
Editorial support by DBePub.com
Illustrations by Gwynne Kerens
Typesetting by HowToTap.com
Printed in USA
First Edition

10 9 8 7 6 5 4 3 2 1

Disclaimer

Please read the following before proceeding:

The information presented in this coursebook entitled *EFT Level 2 Comprehensive Training Resource* (the "coursebook"), including ideas, suggestions, techniques, and other materials, is educational in nature and is provided only as general information. The information presented in the coursebook is not intended to create and does not constitute any professional relationship between the reader and the authors and should not be relied upon as medical, psychological, coaching, or other professional advice of any kind or nature whatsoever.

This coursebook contains information regarding an innovative meridian-based healing technique called Emotional Freedom Techniques (EFT). EFT uses the ancient Chinese meridian system with a gentle tapping procedure that stimulates designated meridian end points on the face and body. Although EFT appears to have promising mental, spiritual, and physical benefits, it has yet to be fully researched by the Western academic, medical, and psychological communities and, therefore, is considered experimental. EFT is self-regulated and is considered "alternative" or "complementary" to the healing arts that are licensed in the United States.

Due to the experimental nature of EFT, that it is a relatively new healing approach, and because the extent of EFT's effectiveness, risks, and benefits are not fully known, you agree to assume and accept full responsibility for any and all risks associated with reading this coursebook and using EFT. You understand that if you choose to use EFT, it is possible that emotional or physical sensations or additional unresolved memories may surface, which could be perceived as negative side effects. Emotional material may continue to surface after using EFT, indicating that other issues may need to be addressed. Previously vivid or traumatic memories may fade, which could adversely impact your ability to provide detailed legal testimony regarding a traumatic incident.

EFT is not a substitute for medical or psychological treatment. You agree to consult with your professional health-care provider for any specific medical problem or psychological disorder. In addition, you understand that any information contained in this coursebook is *not* to be considered a recommendation that you stop seeing any of your health-care professionals or taking any prescribed medication, without consulting your health-care professional, even if, after reading this coursebook and using EFT, it appears and indicates that such medication or therapy is unnecessary. The authors strongly advise that you seek professional advice as appropriate before using EFT, before implementing any protocol or opinion expressed in this coursebook, and before making any health decision.

If you intend to use EFT with others, you agree to use EFT only within your prescribed scope of practice, under appropriate ethical guidelines, and to comply with all applicable laws and regulations. Any stories or testimonials contained herein do not constitute a warranty, guarantee, or prediction regarding the outcome of an individual using EFT for any particular issue. Further, you understand the authors make no warranty, guarantee, or prediction regarding any outcome from you using EFT for any particular issue. While all materials and links to other resources are posted in good faith, the accuracy, validity, effectiveness, completeness, or usefulness of any information herein, as with any publication, cannot be guaranteed. The authors accept no responsibility or liability whatsoever for the use or misuse of the information provided here, including the use of information in links to other resources.

By continuing to read this coursebook you agree to fully release, indemnify, and hold harmless, the authors, their respective heirs, personal representatives, agents, consultants, employees, and assigns from any claim or liability whatsoever and for any damage or injury, personal, financial, emotional, psychological, or otherwise that you may incur, arising at any time out of, or in relation to, your use of the information presented in this coursebook. If any court of law rules that any part of the Disclaimer is invalid, the Disclaimer stands as if those parts were struck out.

By Continuing to Read This Coursebook,
You Agree to All of the Above Disclaimer

Note: This coursebook is the culmination of input from dozens of experienced trainers of EFT. The authors have researched and referenced original EFT writings by Gary Craig to cover level 2 EFT topics in an informative and helpful way, while also attempting to give the reader an overview of some of the more popular modifications that are being used in the field by practitioners around the world. Although you can learn EFT from this coursebook, it is not intended to be a stand-alone training coursebook. Its intent is to complement live training by going into more depth about the use of EFT than any one class can do in the time allotted.

This coursebook is written as a reference book for all serious students of EFT. It is meant as a companion for review after watching DVDs and as reinforcement and review for any level 2 EFT class. It can also be used as a workbook for EFT exercises.

Though actual client cases have been used, names and other identifying information have been changed.

Contents

THE DUNGEON

OPENING THE DOORS TO THE PALACE

About the Authors

Ann Adams

Ann Adams is a licensed clinical social worker with over 35 years of experience in administrative and clinical roles. She began studying EFT in 1999 and has been an active EFT practitioner and trainer ever since. She worked closely with the creator of EFT, Gary Craig. She presented on Craig's EFT Specialty Series I DVD on "Modifying EFT for Use with Emotionally Disturbed Children" and "Getting EFT Accepted by Institutions." She worked closely with him to develop training guidelines, and then served as Director of his EFT Masters Program, finally receiving EFTCert-Honors in Craig's last EFT practitioner certification program.

Ann still maintains a small EFT caseload, but now specializes in "helping the helpers." She is a DCEP with Association of Comprehensive Energy Practitioners (ACEP) and was the first American to receive Training of Trainers certification from the Association for the Advancement of Meridian Energy Techniques (AAMET). She has presented EFT topics at many conferences including ACEP, National Association of Social Workers-Georgia Chapter (NASW-GA) and the EFT Masterclass in the UK.

www.FromTheDeskofAnnAdams.com

Karin Davidson

Karin Davidson is a certified hypnotherapist, a Reiki master, an EFT Trainer, the first Matrix Reimprinting Trainer in the US, and co-founder of the Meridian Tapping Techniques Association. Karin began her career as a professional TV Producer and host who now uses her talents to help spread EFT to the world. She has videotaped and produced over 100 training DVDs for 28 of the 29 EFT Masters, EFT founder Gary Craig, Matrix Reimprinting trainers, TAT founder Tapas Fleming, Ask & Recieve founder Sandi Radomski, *The Secret's* Bob Doyle, *Meta-Medicine's* Richard Flook, and more.

Karin is a sought-after speaker, known for her humor, clarity, and insights. She speaks on EFT and Matrix Reimprinting on the radio, television, and internet, and she maintains a private EFT practice. She also helped develop the curriculum for EFT training for EFT Universe and MTT, update the curriculum for AAMET (Association for the Advancement of Meridian Energy Techniques) and currently trains EFT for AAMET.

www.HowToTap.com

Foreword

By Dr. Patricia Carrington, EFT Founding Master

The challenge of writing a manual for Level 2 EFT training is not to be taken lightly. This is especially true today when so much information has accrued in the field since the time EFT's founder, Gary Craig, wrote his original manual for this method. Fortunately, Ann Adams and Karin Davidson, the authors of this book, have triumphed over the many difficulties involved and have produced a truly valuable and authoritative guide to the clinical use of EFT.

I have always been interested in the challenge of teaching EFT Level 2 where we move from the basic practices taught in Level 1 up to where we begin to apply EFT clinically. The trick here is to keep the all-important foundational teaching while highlighting appropriate innovation. This is not easily done, but it is exactly what the authors of this book have accomplished so impressively. They keep you at all times on track and organized.

They also keep you interested and involved as you read the book – which is really a feat for a manual. I usually look upon a coursebook as a somewhat dry, necessarily obsessive, tome. This manual is detailed to be sure, but with just the right amount of detail. It never distracts you with unnecessary information nor repeats dry facts. It does not weigh you down with unnecessary passing fads or less than important innovations. It remains with what is important and clarifies it admirably.

The authors also give examples – a plethora of them. I love to see really good examples used in a teaching format. With them, the content becomes alive and meaningful.

The result is a book that can be relied upon to be used to teach EFT to others – easily, effectively and with clinical acumen. The Adams-Davidson manual is clear, precise and solid.

I am particularly impressed by what they have accomplished because I remember what the field was like at its inception when I read Dr. Roger Callahan's first book on meridian tapping (*The Five Minute Phobia Cure*). The book did not have a very convincing title, I must admit, but I was startled by the effectiveness of the method it taught. "Tapping" literally revolutionized my practice as a clinical psychologist because I could suddenly do things for people that I had never been able to do before, not even been able to approach, during my traditional practice as a psychotherapist.

I soon found myself developing a simplified, single-algorithm approach that was much easier to teach and administer than Roger's. I called it *Acutap* and taught it to numerous people for almost eight years until I discovered Gary

Craig's EFT method. I soon collapsed my Acutap method into Gary's *Emotional Freedom Techniques* (EFT) and the rest is history.

I want to thank Ann and Karin for their diligent work, their unfailing accuracy of detail, and for the integrity and balanced tone they manage to maintain throughout the book. These things are not only essential to me as a professional but also, more importantly, add to the respect with which our field will be viewed in the future.

As today's up-to-date and authoritative training manual for EFT's Level 2, this book stands unchallenged.

Patricia Carrington, PhD
EFT Founding Master
Clinical Professor, UMDNJ-Robert Wood Johnson Medical School
www.masteringeft.com

Introduction

Welcome to EFT Level 2

If you've studied level 1, you've learned the basic techniques for using EFT to enhance your life, and now you want to go further. You may be especially inspired to expand your use of this tool to help others free themselves of the emotional, physical, or behavioral issues that limit their lives. In level 2, you'll learn techniques that will allow you to begin working with others as well as more advanced ways to use EFT for self-care.

Important Note

Although all trainers attempt to follow EFT training guidelines, trainers have different levels of experience and training in EFT and may have studied other modalities as well. Each trainer tends to emphasize different parts of EFT practices, based on individual preferences and experiences. This book draws on the original writings of EFT's founder, developed curricula from top practitioners, guidelines of the field's professional organizations, and the extensive combined experience of the authors to compile and clarify a comprehensive standard for intermediate EFT training.

That being said, though you can certainly learn a great deal about EFT from books, including this one, keep in mind that it is essential to practice tapping and to attend interactive workshops to *experience* EFT. This coursebook is written as a companion reference guide for level 2 EFT workshops. The tapping experience is highly important. Learning from a book alone is not sufficient if you intend to use EFT with others.

The Foundation

This level 2 text assumes you are familiar with all the concepts from level 1. Although this book builds on concepts from level 1, it does not repeat many of those concepts in detail. Chapter 1 opens with a convenient review, but if you're a little rusty on your level 1 knowledge, consider taking all the Test Your Knowledge quizzes in *EFT Level 1 Comprehensive Training Resource* as a quick refresher before beginning on level 2. Either way, you will want to keep your level 1 material handy to refer to as needed.

You should know:
- *Who are some of the main contributors to the historical development of EFT?*
- *What is the EFT Discovery Statement?*
- *What are meridians and how are they used in EFT?*
- *Name two things that need to be done before beginning to tap.*
- *What points are used in EFT's Basic Recipe?*
- *What is a "Reminder Phrase" and how is it used?*
- *What is meant by "testing" and what are two methods of testing?*
- *List the steps of the Full Basic Recipe.*
- *What is the purpose of the 9 Gamut Procedure?*
- *What are "aspects" of an issue? Give an example of three aspects that might be found for a common phobia, such as a fear of flying.*
- *How do using investigative reporter questions, (i.e., who, what, why...) help to uncover aspects?*
- *Why is it important to be specific and what are some circumstances in which you would NOT want to be specific?*
- *What is the most obvious difference between the Movie Technique and Tell the Story?*
- *What is "Borrowing Benefits"?*
- *What are "Reversals"?*

Chapter 1 – Points

Chapter 1 – Points

The Basic Points

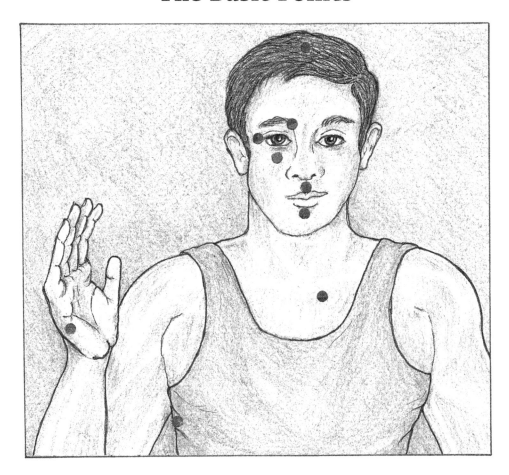

To help you review the points you learned in level 1, here is a chart of both the Basic Recipe (formerly referred to as "the Shortcut") and the Full Basic Recipe, including the 9 Gamut Procedure.

Basic Recipe:
EB – Beginning of Eyebrow
SE – Side of the Eye
UE – Under the Eye
UN – Under the Nose
Ch – Chin
CB – Collarbone
UA – Under Arm
H – Top of Head

Full Basic Recipe:
H – top of head
EB – eyebrow
SE – side of eye
UE – under eye
UN – under nose
Ch – just above chin
CB – collarbone
UA – under arm
BN – below nipple
Th – thumb
IF – index finger
MF – middle finger
BF – baby finger
KC – side of hand

While tapping on the Gamut point:
1. Close your eyes.
2. Open your eyes.
3. Look hard down right to the floor while still holding your head straight ahead.
4. Look hard down left to the floor while still holding your head straight ahead.
5. Roll your eyes in a circle.
6. Roll your eyes in a circle in the opposite direction.
7. Hum about two seconds of any song or melody.
8. Count from one to five.
9. Hum about two seconds of any song or melody again.

H – top of head
EB – eyebrow
SE – side of eye
UE – under eye
UN – under nose
Ch – just above chin
CB – collarbone
UA – under arm
BN – below nipple
Th – thumb
IF – index finger
MF – middle finger
BF – baby finger
KC – side of hand

"Your" Point

We stated in level 1 that you might have one point, *your point,* that seems more effective. It's possible that, when you tap your point, you will feel your energy shift. Your point might always be the same point or it could change at times.

Don't be concerned if you don't have a point or if you can't feel your energy shifts. This, too, is normal. Ask yourself or your client if either of you felt more of a release or shift on any one point. If one point is more helpful than other points, use it. If that point gives no relief, move on to other points.

Many people report that they use specific points for specific things during their daily lives. For example:

- *Tapping on the Collarbone point while watching something disturbing on television*
- *Tapping on the Chin point when opening and reading an e-mail that could be upsetting*
- *Lightly squeezing the index finger when nervous*
- *Tapping the top of the head when having trouble getting motivated*

Try different points for different daily annoyances or challenges and see what feels right for you. Remember that negative reactions to daily occurrences also provide an opportunity to note issues that can be worked on later in a full EFT session.

Top of Head Point

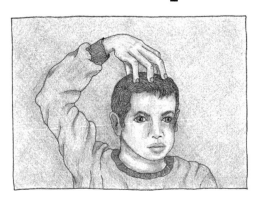

In level 1, we also incorporated the Top of the Head point. Although Craig didn't include it originally, it's now in common usage. This point is at the apex of the head and is called DU 20, *Baihui*, or "Hundred Meetings." As the meeting point of many meridians, it's a powerful contact point for many issues. The point can be found by placing the heel of one hand on the hairline at the forehead and the heel of the other hand at the hairline at the neck. Extend the hands toward each other and the *Baihui* is in a slight depression about an inch behind where the tips of the fingers meet.

Additional Points

Wrist Point

The wrist point (P6, Pericardium 6, *NeiGuan*, or "Inner Gate") is located on the inside of the wrist, the width of three fingers up from the wrist crease. The wrist point covers the upper yin channels – lungs, pericardium, and heart. Since the meridians in the hand run through the wrist, there are additional points on the back of the wrist area as well. To insure all these meridians are involved, both the front and back of the wrist should be tapped. You may note some EFT practitioners using variations. Some use the inside of one wrist to tap the other wrist. Others tap the wrist crease itself, rather than the indicated spot three fingers above it. Fortunately, EFT is a very forgiving system.

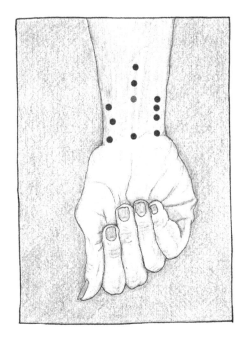

Ankle Points

The *Sanyinjiao*, "Three Yin Intersection," point is located on the inside of the leg, four fingers' width above the medial malleolus, the prominent bone on the inside of the ankle. If you place four fingers at the top of this anklebone, the *Sanyinjiao* point is the slight, sometimes slightly tender, depression you find just as your fourth finger slips off the tibia (the long shin bone). This ankle point covers the lower yin meridians – liver, kidney and spleen, and pancreas. Since this point can be used to induce and ease labor, we recommend that pregnant women avoid using it.

Opposite the *Sanyinjiao*, on the outside of the leg is GB 39, *Xuanzhong*, "Hanging Bell." Tap on both sides of the leg. Some practitioners report that the ankle points are favorites with their male clients.

Gandy's Alternative

Tapping the top of the head, wrist, and both sides of the ankle addresses thirteen of the fourteen meridians. Michael Gandy in *Steps Toward Becoming the Ultimate Therapist*, with Gary Craig, recommended these three points as an EFT shortcut (pp. 9–10). This is useful when working with brief group demos.

Liver Point

The liver point (Liver 14, *Qimen*, or "Cycle Gate") is between the sixth and seventh ribs, in line with the nipple (for women, it's about where the bra band would be). Craig did not generally use the liver point since it can be awkward for women to find this point in public. Many practitioners feel, however, that addressing the liver meridian is important. If the *Qimen*, the end point of the liver meridian, is difficult to reach, practitioners generally choose to use Liver 13. To locate this point, known as *Zhangmen*, "Completion Gate," place your hand on the soft upper abdomen under your ribs and follow the curve of the ribs down until you reach the floating end of the eleventh rib, approximately at the same level as the belly button but to the side of the body. Liver 13 is found just below and behind this spot.

All the meridian points are connected in some way and tapping on one will affect all the meridians, so don't worry too much about which point should be used for what or be concerned if you or your client leaves out a point.

Additional Techniques

There have been many, many variations to EFT developed over the years. Some add points, change the tapping order, add a step, or leave out steps. Some add breathing or other techniques to the tapping. Gary Craig encouraged experimentation with the process and it lends itself well to modification. Some practitioners feel their variation is faster, or quicker, or more effective, or goes deeper than others. Although it may be the case that a particular variation works well for some, there is no research as to the effectiveness of any variation as compared to EFT. This book is designed to teach the original techniques of EFT, so full instruction of variations is outside its scope. We mention them here so that readers are aware of them and can explore on their own.

Floor to Ceiling Eye Roll

The Floor to Ceiling Eye Roll, reminiscent of the work of Moshe Feldenkrais (1972, 1981), is usually used after EFT rounds, when the intensity is down to a 1 or 2. This technique entails *slowly* rolling the eyes, from looking as far down to the floor as possible to as far up to the ceiling as possible while 1) keeping the head forward and unmoving and 2) tapping on the Gamut point. If you are guiding a client in this procedure, you can hold your index finger out in front of the client and ask the client to follow your finger with his or her eyes.

The Four Point Trauma Clearer

Thought Field Therapy (TFT) offers alternative algorithms for use with various issues. In her Level 2 classes, Gwyneth Moss uses a short cut that is similar to the original TFT trauma algorithm. She calls her shortcut "The Four Point Trauma Clearer." TFT founder, Roger Callahan (1996), described the original algorithm for trauma as having four points: eyebrow, under the eye, under the arm, and the collarbone. After tapping the four points, the client was then instructed to complete the 9 Gamut and repeat the four points. This process was done without words. Unlike EFT, TFT doesn't use language when tapping. Later Callahan expanded the four point algorithm to include additional points.

Anxiety Algorithm (or the ACE in a Hole)

A second common TFT algorithm involves three points for anxiety: under the eye, under the arm, and collarbone. These points can be a quick fix, but sometimes much more is needed. Ann taught the children in the residential program these three points she called their ACE in the hole. She taught them to use these points anywhere, anytime, by scratching under their arms, scratching their chests, and rubbing under their eyes. Yes, these points are out of the order specified by Callahan, but because the premise behind EFT is that the order in which you tap the points doesn't matter, then rearranging the algorithms shouldn't matter either. And guess what? It didn't. The kids could remember it, and it worked just fine.

TAB

In Touch and Breathe (TAB), described by John Diepold, instead of tapping each point, you hold each point lightly while taking a slow deep breath.

Stealthy Tapping

This is the name Ann gives to using EFT in public where it may be awkward to tap. There are many creative ways to stimulate the points without actually tapping them. It's beneficial to teach your clients to use this in their everyday lives. It uses the "common touches" you normally use anyway such as scratching the top of your head, rubbing between your eyebrows, rubbing under your eyes, tapping your fingers, and resting your hand on your chest. When this is done slowly as you take a couple of slow breaths, it is not noticeable to those around you. You also may notice that one or more points have a more calming effect than others. Try just using those. A common use of Stealthy Tapping is in work meetings where you can rub the finger points while holding your hands out of sight beneath a conference table.

Continuous Tapping

Australian clinical psychologists Steve Wells and David Lake use a version of continuous tapping. In this variation, users tap continuously while telling their stories. This technique is especially useful for beginners or when emotions are running high. Continuous tapping is useful when a client simply wants to "vent." You can help clients when they pause, by repeating last words as a question. "You felt used?" "You wanted to scream?" Clients will normally say yes and continue venting. Anyone can tap while voicing feelings. Many practitioners have their clients continuously tap on a chosen point in between actual EFT rounds. This can help clients focus and help bring up events and feelings related to the discussion.

Simplified Energy Techniques (SET)

SET is another technique developed by Wells and Lake that doesn't require a Setup or Reminder, doesn't use the 9 Gamut, and doesn't deal with reversals.

Tapas Acupressure Technique (TAT)

In EFT, we strive to use specific feelings, emotions, and events. Tapas Fleming developed TAT to address issues that are more general. This is useful when a client has difficulty pinpointing one event or has had the same problem for many years and it seems "too big." Often EFTers will use TAT to lower overall intensity and then use traditional EFT to get to the specifics.

Deciding Not to Tap

Other practitioners feel that continuous tapping can, at times, be distracting, especially when clients may just need to talk. A basic human need is, after all, to have someone truly listen and work to understand. Clients who have never before shared their stories may need just to be listened to with full acceptance, without judgment or expectations of any kind – including without the expectation that they tap. Some practitioners tell their clients, "I'll tap for you as you talk." This can be a supportive gesture and is often appreciated in these cases. As always, use your clinical judgment when choosing any technique.

Chapter 2 – Testing

Testing – Review of Level 1

Testing is extremely important in EFT. As with other therapeutic modalities, after a session you may ask what the client gained during the session. Or ask for feedback: "Are we on the right track with what we are doing?"

EFT can uncover many aspects of an issue and can resolve issues so quickly that without testing it would often be unclear what's been covered in a session.

Testing is used to
- *Give the practitioner confidence that everything has been sufficiently cleared,*
- *Give clients confidence that they can now face issues in real life from a different perspective,*
- *See if clients can now do what they couldn't do before.*

There is no testing better than the real-life experience and reactions the client has between sessions, but we have many techniques for subjective measurement during a session.

Measuring Intensity Levels

Intensity levels are taken after tapping rounds to assess movement on the issue. This measure also helps you know where to start and can suggest which EFT technique to use to address the problem. Your ideal starting place for directly addressing a specific issue is mid-range intensity and below. High-range intensity, 8 to 10, should be handled in a more general way before getting specific.

Let's review the various methods for measuring intensity you learned in level 1.

Subjective Units of Distress (SUD) Scale

Most commonly used is a 0 – 10 scale. You ask clients where they are on the scale as a measure of intensity. Karin often says, "Zero is that it doesn't bother you at all, and 10 is if you want to run screaming out of the room." If someone is very upset and gives you a number well over 10 to emphasize how much, appreciate that the person is in touch with her feelings and go with it. The importance of taking a measurement is just to show change; there's no need to adhere to any specific system.

If a person starts out very upset and it does not seem appropriate to ask, assume she is at a 10 and start tapping. After the client calms, ask, "If you were a 10 when we started, what is your intensity now?"

Percentage

Measuring changes in percentages from 0 to 100 percent is also useful in assessing the "truth" or level of belief in a statement, in lieu of the Validity of Cognition scale (see later). For example, if a client says, "I can't hold onto money," you can ask how true that statement feels.

Outstretched Hands

The scale for measuring in this way is arms out as far as possible equals a 10 and hands together in a prayer position equals a 0. Ann finds this especially useful with children.

Metaphor

For this measure, use a metaphor such as a traffic light: red, yellow, green. Child-relevant metaphors can be papa bear, mama bear, or baby bear size.

Additional Testing Methods

Validity of Cognition (VOC) Scale

This tool can be used to measure the level of belief of any statement using a scale from 1 to 7, with 1 being false, 4 being neutral, and 7 being true. You can ask your client, for example, "How true is the statement 'I'm okay now'?"

You can use the 1 to 7 scale for such questions as "How much truth is in that thought/belief?" or "How much doubt is in that statement?"

Submodalities

If you are familiar with Neuro-Linguistic Programming (NLP), you will recognize some of the NLP concepts embedded within EFT. Gary Craig was a NLP Master Practitioner prior to developing EFT. "Submodalities" is an NLP term for the aspects of the five senses we use to code our experiences. We use our five senses when we describe our experiences to others.

For example, in observing a recent accident, you might describe the experience as visual, "The bright lights were so close"; auditory, "The noise was overwhelming"; kinesthetic, "I could feel my skin crawl with fear"; olfactory, "The smell of the gasoline was overpowering"; or gustatory, "I could taste the dust in the air."

We also use the five senses to describe our internal experiences – the "pictures in our head." We use these codes to help us identify how we feel about our experiences. Our emotions can be affected by the submodalities we use and, in turn, when the emotion changes, the submodality is affected by those emotional changes as well.

EFT uses the concept of submodalities to gain clarity around a specific memory before tapping to relieve the emotion attached to that memory. Submodalities can help people describe the "movie" of their event, or to help describe their pain or their physical experience as they use the Tell the Story technique. We'll discuss submodalities in more detail in the section on these techniques.

The Dungeon

Gary Craig, the founder of EFT, used a powerful metaphor for the way our beliefs affect our lives. He wrote, in an early series of articles for his website, which he later collected into the book *Palace of Possibilities: Using EFT to Achieve One's Potential,* that we all live in a "palace of possibilities" with many, many rooms, with unlimited options and potential. All the rooms are open to each of us, and yet many of us only live our lives in a few of our rooms. Craig opens the series with the idea that, in fact, many people live in the dungeons of their palaces and that much of conventional psychological care is limited to helping people out of the dungeon. EFT, on the other hand, is capable of helping people to explore and enjoy their entire wonderful palace.

If someone is living in the dungeon, it means there is still such a high charge of intensity around an event or issue that it seriously affects that person's ability to function fully and happily. In addition, and, perhaps, more importantly, the level of upset around an issue may make it very difficult for the person to discuss the issue because it's too upsetting. One of the great advantages of EFT is that it does not require anyone to relive emotional pain or trauma. In fact, it is not even necessary for you to know what a client's issue is in order to use EFT to help. It's the client's knowledge and focus that is important, not yours. If a client is in the dungeon, still experiencing a high level of upset, EFT can help reduce the intensity around an issue with a number of gentle techniques.

Chapter 3 – Peace Without Pain

The great beauty of EFT is that it uses simple tools to address issues as easily and painlessly as possible. Unlike the popular workout advice "No pain, no gain," we don't have to experience *more* pain in order to relieve the pain that old issues are causing us. Many forms of traditional therapy involve having to reexperience the trauma in some way. For example, some aversion or immersion therapies require incremental or excessive exposure to triggers in order to anesthetize or acclimate the patient to the stimulus.

In fact, there is a current, well-accepted therapy of this type that shares the initials of Emotional Freedom Techniques. Your clients who are new to EFT may be confused if they've heard of Emotionally Focused Therapies, in which clients are required to relive emotions in order to transform them. The technique has gained a good reputation for use in couple's counseling. Although the name is similar, the philosophy is completely different. You can assure your clients that, no, they will not need to relive the pain of the past in order to move on to their future. Whether your clients have high intensity around an issue, aren't ready to talk about an issue, or don't even consciously recognize the issue, EFT has a battery of techniques you can use to approach the problem to get them out of their "dungeon."

In fact, a great deal of EFT practice is matching the technique, not only to the type of issue the client has, but also to the client's intensity level as the issue is addressed. We will return to this concept again and again, discussing how to choose or adjust a technique depending on the emotional intensity the client feels at that moment about that issue.

You learned something of the Watch the Movie and Tell the Story techniques in level 1, but sometimes clients need a more "distant" or "gentler" technique before they can make use of more direct, specific ones. Three EFT techniques – Tearless Trauma, Sneaking Up on the Problem, and Chasing the Pain – are categorized as "Gentle Techniques" because they work to decrease or prevent the emotional intensity around an issue.

Tearless Trauma Technique

The distinguishing feature of the Tearless Trauma Technique is that clients do *not* focus directly on their feelings or reactions to the issue, rather, they *guess* what the intensity *would* be *if* the issue were to be the focus. In level 1, you learned how to use the Tearless Trauma Technique when working with individuals.

Gary Craig (1999) originally developed the technique in public group settings where he was amazed at its effectiveness in reducing the intensity levels for groups who had experienced serious trauma, even though the members did not share details of the events with Craig. In other words, they did not need to relive the event in order to feel relief. After using this technique for some time, Craig reintroduced the steps, adding commentary that emphasizes his attitude about the needlessness of introducing emotional pain into a session. His words further illuminate the utility of the Gentle Techniques:

> I don't see why pain is at all necessary... I have taken care of a mountain of traumatic incidents ... and, after the healing...the client seems done with the issue because the resolution that is so highly valued by the more intense techniques seems to take place within the EFT session with minimal pain. To me, this is profound and tempts me to rename the process "Peace without Pain." As long as I get the resolution without the pain, then I don't see the need for the pain.

The Peace without Pain name never seems to have caught on, but Craig's steps for Tearless Trauma have not changed:

1. Ask the participants to identify a specific traumatic incident from their past. Ask that it be at least three years ago to minimize any complications from the dynamics of a current event. An example might be, "the time my father punched me when I was 12." By contrast, the phrase "my father abused me" would be too broad because, chances are, the abuse took place over many, many incidents. Please note that you may need to instruct clients to stay on their original issue because many of them will shift to other issues as they resolve the original one.

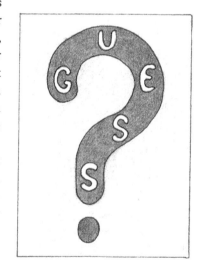

2. Ask the participants to *guess* what their emotional intensity would be (on a 0-10 scale) *if* they were to vividly imagine the incident. Instruct them *not* to actually imagine it (although some will close their eyes and do this anyway). This guess is a surprisingly useful estimate, and it serves to minimize emotional pain. Have them write down their guesses, and then go around the room having them state their number. This gives you a good feel for various participants' intensity.

3. Have the participants develop a phrase to use for the EFT process such as "this father-punch emotion" and then proceed with a round of tapping.

4. After this round of tapping, ask them to guess again, and go around the room asking them to state their new number. Typically, they report noticeably smaller numbers.

5. Perform more rounds of EFT (or your favorite tapping procedure). Go around the room after each time, asking for their new numbers. In my experience, a total of three or four rounds will bring just about everyone down to guesses of 0 to 3.

6. Once everyone is down to acceptably low guesses, then perform another round of tapping and, after this round, ask them to vividly imagine the incident. Notice that this is the first time you are asking them to do this. All previous times have been relatively painless guesses. In my experience, just about everyone goes to 0 and the rest are at very low numbers. If there is an exception or two, then work with them individually to complete the process. (Craig, 1999)

With this technique, you ask your clients (or in a workshop, your audience or participants) to *guess* at what the intensity would be *if* they were to tune in to the event. Have them give the event a name. Tap using their event name. Keep tapping on the event, until the guessed intensity is a 3 or lower. Then try going to the Movie Technique.

Tearless Trauma is not always tearless. Craig called it that because he witnessed very little emotional upset when using it. The central difference between this and another technique, however, is that you do not ask the participant to imagine the event in detail until *after* the emotional upset has already been reduced. Going back into the traumatic event and strong emotion is *not* necessary to resolve an issue. With EFT, *you do not have to relive your issue to release or resolve it.*

Sneaking Up on the Problem

"Sneaking Up" doesn't deal with any event directly; it deals with the *fear* of addressing the event directly.

This technique is useful when you already know that

- *Clients will experience very high intensity if the issue is addressed directly.*
- *Clients have high levels of resistance to getting into this issue at all.*
- *Clients will benefit from tapping as early in the process as possible, even while the fear of looking at an issue keeps them from addressing it directly.*

Sneaking Up is *similar* to Tearless Trauma in that the intent is to prevent as much emotional upset as possible. In Sneaking Up, however, you don't want clients to *guess* at any intensity if they were to focus on the issue. You don't want them to focus on the issue *at all*. You are only addressing the existing *fear of* **thinking about** *focusing* on the upsetting event.

Sneaking Up is another distancing technique; that is how it keeps the emotional intensity down. It is, after all, easier to tap for something "out there" than when the pain is directly in front of you. When the fear of "out there" has been reduced, the issue can be moved closer with much less upset.

Sneaking Up will help clients deal with their *fear* of addressing the incident directly when there is an issue that is so overwhelming that, up to this point, they have avoided it in every way possible. To them, it has been beyond help. It's the "Big One" they most fear to touch. It may be an issue that carries heavy guilt or shame or a major trauma they don't want to revisit. Whatever "it" is, they are very anxious or fearful and often unwilling to address it, certainly in a direct manner. Often, simply knowing they don't have to address it will lower their anxiety.

Sometimes a client has spent a great deal of energy, since the event, pushing down the associated feelings and memories. When a person believes the issue cannot be resolved, working to keep the issue below the surface is a logical decision. The problem is that this "Big One" doesn't stay buried; it simmers under the surface until it begins to boil over and influence the client's feelings, thoughts, and responses, interfering with the client's daily life. The client sees the issue as so big, so difficult to deal with, that it seems preferable to live a less-than-truly-functional life rather than come face to face with the issue. In a case like this, rapport with the client is especially important. Until the client trusts you and trusts that EFT could be effective for this "unsolvable" problem, the client will only address the "little stuff" with you and will avoid this major event.

Before clients feel fully safe in their EFT sessions, they often don't even mention this significant event for fear you *will* want to address it. As significant rapport and trust build in your relationships with clients, they begin to feel safe enough to begin to *hint* at this overwhelming issue. They begin to tiptoe around it.

You want to follow your client's lead and tiptoe around, sneaking up on it as well. Timing is important. Strong rapport and deep respect for your client are always important, but they are imperative here. You can help clients by letting them know that keeping this big thing tucked away means it's always there. Wouldn't it be nice to get rid of it, rather than keep storing it and trying to push it down?

When your client is ready and willing to begin just to think about addressing the event (remember when the *client* is ready, not when *you* are), you can begin to address the issue by asking your client to rank the intensity he feels with the mere *thought* of approaching "this Big Event" (or some other representative phrase). Usually the intensity is high with even the mere thought.

When you begin to approach this, pay attention to the client's reactions, and watch for physical manifestations of stress. Don't ask a client to rank the discomfort when it is obvious. If this happens, just start tapping in a very general way to help take the edge off. Use general Setups that address the discomfort, *not* the issue. If a client can rank the discomfort, you might use, "Even though just thinking about dealing with this event, I am an 8, I deeply and completely accept myself." If the client can't even approach that, you might use, "Even though just thinking about dealing with this upsets me..." "Even though I have discomfort about this issue..." "Even though this thing seems too big for me..." "Even though it's easier to pretend it never happened..."

Remember, monitor your client's physical reactions. After reducing the intensity with some very global and vague Setups, you might ask about any physical symptoms. The client may describe a pounding heart, sweating, constricted throat, nausea, or other symptom. Again, don't get into the details of the *event* at all. Use Setups like "Even though my heart is pounding ..." or "Even though it makes my head hurt to consider looking at this..." Alternatively, you can use whatever words your client gives you, "Even though it upsets my tummy just to think about even the possibility of dealing with this event..."

Do several rounds of EFT until you see some signs of relaxation. One common clue to reduced intensity is a deep breath or sigh, but you may see a variety of physiological changes. Whatever you see, assure your client all reactions are normal. When the client is calmer, test progress by asking the client to repeat a code word, such as "the Big One," and re-rank intensity. When both emotional responses and physical symptoms are reduced, you will note the resistance to dealing with the issue decreases as well.

Keep repeating tapping sequences and general Setups until it seems appropriate to ask, "Is there any part of this issue that you *could* talk about comfortably?" If there is, address the part the client brings up. If talking brings up intensity, use general tapping to take the edge off, then get more detailed.

Generally, even when the discomfort lessens, there is still emotional discomfort when dealing with the issue directly. Just keep tapping, using vague, related statements ("Even though I have this emotion...") until the intensity is lower. When the intensity is very low, then you can begin to address actual parts of the issue until, finally, resistance to addressing the issue lowers and the client is able to use the Tell the Story or Watch the Movie Techniques. Remember, the client wants resolution. If you can have resolution without pain, there's no need for the pain. Your job is to keep the process moving toward resolution as painlessly as possible.

There are a number of circumstances when you will find Sneaking Up on the Problem to be useful. For example, there may be times when a client is highly emotional about an issue and you don't want the client even to attempt to guess at the intensity. You can first deal with the anxiety around dealing with an issue and then decrease surrounding emotions before addressing the issue directly.

You'll also find Sneaking Up useful when the client's life is organized around having a particular issue. You will want to address the issue in very small steps. As with Tearless Trauma, Sneaking Up is useful with group trauma such as was experienced after 9/11 or Hurricane Katrina.

You might use Sneaking Up when there's not enough time to address an issue fully; however, in that case, you should consider the wisdom of starting on the "Big One" at all. As always, err on the side of caution. Slow and conservative is best.

Karin Davidson has had clients who have come to her when someone close to them has died and, in their words, they "can't seem to go on," and can't "handle the pain." Sometimes they can't articulate much more than this. Karin begins by helping them identify the impact of the loss, whatever they *are* able to talk about: the meaning the loss has in their lives, the feelings around being home alone, feeling lost, having no purpose, not wanting to go back to work – anything other than the death itself. She may even focus on how they would *like* to feel instead.

Suggesting that you use EFT with a generic statement such as "these issues" or that you use distancing or gentle techniques may seem as if we are suggesting avoiding the "real" issue. However, working on the emotions that are the result of an event without going directly to dealing with that event can help clients ease into more intense emotions.

We are not suggesting that people should not feel the "normal" emotions that one would expect to feel after a trauma. For instance, it is entirely normal for people to need a grieving period after the loss of a loved one. The time they take to grieve and the way grief is expressed will be different for each individual. At no time does EFT take away normal, natural emotions and reactions to tragic events. EFT only helps to take away the "over the top" emotions that interfere with a person's ability to deal with issues. EFT is supremely useful in dealing with unhealthy reactions.

A healthy reaction to misfortune, loss, mistreatment, or disaster is a reaction to the *event*. A healthy person recognizes that the *event* was bad. An unhealthy reaction is one in which a person interprets that the bad event means the *person* is bad. It's a reaction that adds a limiting belief about the self or the world to the "writing on the walls." This is the way people end up carrying traumatic events with them throughout their lives. EFT can help clients remove this sort of "emotional baggage." When it does, they may even find that expressing their natural human reactions is easier.

Chasing the Pain

In level 1, you learned about Chasing the Pain as a technique to use when physical symptoms move around the body. Another context for the use of Chasing the Pain is as one of the Gentle Techniques.

You always want to observe carefully when you are working with a client. In the section on Sneaking Up, we discussed the importance of watching for a client's physical reactions. This can be especially helpful when we wish to be on guard against raising emotional intensity too high or when a client can't articulate the problem. People may not recall a traumatic memory, but their *bodies* do. Be aware that, while our conscious minds try to fool us or work to hide things we don't want to see, "the body never lies." Our bodies can still show us what's really going on.

When clients are not ready or not able to identify emotions around an issue, they may be able to begin to work on an issue by first identifying where they feel the emotion in the body. A client who is unable or unwilling to talk about the emotions around being rejected by a parent may be able to identify clearly a hard knot in the pit of the stomach.

William James, who established the first laboratory of experimental psychology at Harvard in 1875, expounded one of the first theories that emotion arises from physical feelings in the body: "When worried...the focus of one's... consciousness is the contraction...of the eyes and brows. When...embarrassed, it is something in the pharynx that compels...a swallow, a clearing of the throat, or a...cough.... If we fancy some strong emotion, and then...abstract from our consciousness...all the...bodily symptoms, we find we have nothing left behind, no 'mind-stuff' out of which the emotion can be constituted." In other words, according to James, emotion *is* the feeling in the body, or, at any rate, the interpretation the brain makes of the feeling in the body. It stands to reason that relieving the discomfort in the body will help to relieve the emotional discomfort as well.

Note: With the severely disturbed population in the residential program for children and adolescents where Ann worked, she usually got faster cooperation, with fewer objections, by asking an upset child, "Where do you feel the upset in your body?" When they told her where and what, she asked how bad the body feeling was. They then used EFT on the body feeling. As they told Ann that the body feeling was relieved, she would also note they were no longer upset. People don't always know exactly what is bothering them or where the negative emotion is coming from. Most people, however, can give you a description of how their bodies are feeling.

Tapping for the *body's reaction* to the emotion around a trauma is generally more indirect and, therefore, often gentler, than using specific words about a traumatic event. If you feel this is appropriate for your client, guide the client to create a Setup that represents the answer to the question, "Where do you feel this emotion in your body?"

Although, in this case, when using Gentle Techniques, you may be avoiding getting specific about the underlying issue or traumatic event, if possible, be specific about describing the body feeling, the physiological reaction.

Ask questions to help the client give as much detail as possible:
- *Where exactly is the feeling in your body?*
- *What type of feeling is it?*
- *How intense is the feeling?*

- *Can you describe the feeling: is it pressure, or like a ball, or a cloud, or a weight?*

If the physical issue is chronic, not simply a temporary emotional response, it may be helpful to use the actual diagnosis or ways the problem is affecting the body as well. We will discuss dealing with physical issues in more detail later in the book.

Note: Always remember that, although EFT can be very effective with physical issues, if a client asks you for help with an ongoing physical problem, make sure the client has first had the problem assessed by a physician. *Unless you are a physician yourself, you should never address serious physical issues or chronic pain without a medical diagnosis.* In addition, some locales consider the treating of pain or even advertising that you address any medical condition to be practicing medicine without a license. Be careful in your marketing of your services. EFT "addresses energy imbalances in the body." It does not "treat" medical issues or pain.

In Sneaking Up on the Problem, we mentioned such possible Setups as "Even though my heart is pounding ..." or "Even though it makes my head hurt to consider looking at this..." or "Even though it upsets my tummy just to think about it...." So what is the dif-

ference between that and what we do in Chasing the Pain? Sneaking Up is used primarily to address the *fear* of looking at an issue. Chasing the Pain, when used in this context as a Gentle Technique, is for when emotions can't be articulated, but a physiological reaction can. (Chasing the Pain can, of course, also be used to address actual physical issues, but that is a different application. We'll look a bit more at that in the section on physical issues.)

When tapping for tension or pain in the body or for any physiological reaction, it's very common for the pain or discomfort to seem to migrate from one place in the body to another as you tap. The mechanism for this is complex but interesting. Just as emotion is our brain's perception of certain feelings in our bodies, pain is only our brain's perception of stronger stimuli. The neurological mechanism for the brain's perception of pain, or nociception, causes pain to be perceived at different levels and in two different stages. Pain receptors can only perceive stimuli that are above a certain strength and each stimulus is sent to the brain in two stages. The first, faster stage allows the brain to locate the pain. The slower second stage allows it to assess it. When a strong pain is perceived, a weaker one will be ignored. In addition, the pain perception can be interrupted or confused by simultaneous non-painful stimuli. So, rubbing a stubbed toe makes it feel better because the rubbing interferes with the brain's reception of the stronger painful stimuli. Likewise, as long as the toe hurts, you won't notice that you also bumped your knee. When the toe feels better, the pain will "move" to the knee. (Apkarian, Hashmi, Baliki, 2011) In short, for our purposes, when the pain "moves," we follow the pain wherever it goes, thus "Chasing the Pain."

The pain may move or it may change in its presentation or intensity. For example, you may start the Setup with a general statement, "this migraine pain," and revise to a more specific Reminder Phrase, "this sharp eye pain," then revise again to "this eye twinge," to "this neck discomfort," to "this tightness and heavy feeling in my shoulders."

Judy started out tapping for her hip pain. But the pain moved to her lower back, so she thought EFT wasn't working for her since she still had pain. This movement is actually a good sign. When EFT effects *any* change in the pain, this is a sign that EFT *is* working. Continue to chase the pain, however it changes or moves. As you see improvement, test your client's progress by asking the client to go back to the originally reported physical sensation.

As clients calm by tapping on the physical manifestations of their issues, watch for signs that they are ready to talk about the event or to move on to more specific techniques such as the Watch the Movie or Tell the Story Techniques.

Dealing with the Extremes

The point of learning and using the Gentle Techniques is, of course, to avoid provoking intense and painful emotion in your clients. However, as we all know, "the best-laid plans…" You must be prepared to act appropriately in case a client does experience very high intensity.

High Intensity

As we've discussed, if a person is in the highest range of intensity (SUD 8-10) on an issue, you want to use the gentler techniques to bring down the intensity *before* getting into any details. Remember, while specificity is of utmost importance, trust the process; EFT works even when sneaking up on the problem or tapping very generally. Don't rush clients into being specific if they're already upset.

In the worst cases, just tap without words. Words are *not* necessary for EFT to have a calming effect – just tap. Generally, when such high intensity exists, if you have permission, it may be best to tap *on* the person. Make sure you have permission. If someone is in a highly emotional state, beginning to tap on them unexpectedly could create additional problems. Always ask. A very gentle and less invasive method is to start tapping on the points on their hands, using the finger points or hold their hands gently as you press the Karate Chop point and Gamut point at the same time.

An important principle is distancing, or dissociation. There are various methods for helping clients keep at a "distance" from an issue. Two basic principles for distancing are either vagueness or distraction. You can be very general in talking about "the thing" or be very specific in talking about something other than "the thing." One distancing method, adapted from NLP, is movie theater visualization. You ask the client to picture a calm, quiet, comfortable theater with cozy seats. The event is on the screen, which is behind a thick, heavy curtain. Have the client sit where he's most comfortable, up front, in the middle, the back, or coming into the projector room, for instance. A client can visualize you or anyone else sitting with him. Here, you can begin by using the client's own language for the event or tap using a generic description such as some variation of "Even though that awful movie is playing behind that thick curtain, I realize I am safe in the audience with ___ and I'm okay." The Reminder Phrase would be the very general "That awful movie."

Put It in a Box

Another way is to have the client imagine putting the issue in a box with a lid. Have the client describe the box. You can use very general language as you did with the "awful movie," or you might use the opposite technique, getting very, very specific about the box. The lid can fasten or not; the material of the box can vary; the box can have locks or not. If needed, put that box into another box and describe the second box.

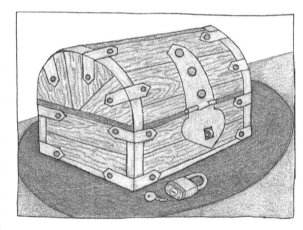

Once the issue is safely inside a well-described box, tap, using some variation of "Even though I have something in this small black lacquer wooden box with gold locks and short round stubby legs..." Continue tapping on just the description of the outer box until the intensity around opening the outermost box is low enough that the client can visualize taking the lid off that box, then tap for the next box. You can tap on what the box looks like – its color and shape. You can even put the box in a trash bag and have the trash truck come and take it to the dump. You can even put the box on another planet. Keep tapping until the client can have the box in the room or can think about the *possibility* of opening the box. When intensity is lower, ask if the client can open the box. Then tap using the Tell the Story or Watch the Movie Technique.

When clients begin to get highly upset, they often close their eyes; keep tapping and have them open their eyes and look at you. You do not want them to close their eyes and go further into the event. When we are highly emotional, we tend to "curl up" and close our eyes. Seeing the strong reactions of someone reliving a traumatic event can be unnerving to the practitioner, so be sure to stay calm yourself.

Speak calmly, quietly, and firmly. You can say gently, "Look at me." In some instances (again, with permission), you may want to gently raise their chin to help them direct their attention to looking at you. Keeping them "in the room, in the now" with you will prevent them from associating back into the trauma in the "there and then."

In the case of a true abreaction, in which a client does not calm after a few minutes of tapping, you'll need to dissociate the client from the emotion. Keep tapping and directing him back to the here and now. Help him see that he's safe and sitting in the chair in the room with you. Ask the client to tell you where he is; remind him to look at you, ask distracting questions like "What's the color of the carpet?" or "What did you have for breakfast?" Ask the client to stand up with you and move. Wait until intensity drops or for another session before moving on to any other techniques.

No Measurable Intensity

Working effectively with EFT does not *require* an emotional charge. EFT still works if the reported emotional intensity is 0. However, you do want clients to be tuned in. Even without intensity, you need an awareness of the incident while telling about the issue or memory.

Sometimes people feel little or no emotion when an emotional reaction would be appropriate. These people are so adept at dissociation (distancing themselves from the problem or memory) that they may not be able to detect their own feelings around a negative incident. This may seem like a positive. If the problem isn't bothering you, why consider it a problem? These people may come to you because they know something is bothering them. They see evidence in addictive behaviors or poor choices, for instance, but they have difficulty identifying what's upsetting them because they don't feel upset. In these cases, ask them to tell you how they know they don't feel anything. Focus on how much they are *not* feeling. Often you can create Setups from these answers. For instance, a client might answer, "I know I don't feel anything, because last time I broke up with my girlfriend, I couldn't concentrate on work, I kept wanting to call her. But this time, I feel nothing." An effective Setup might be "Even though, last time I couldn't concentrate, but this time I feel nothing, I deeply and completely accept myself anyway." Feelings and details will often arise while tapping on the lack of feeling.

This is what happened when Sam came to see Karin with very low to no measurable intensity in his affect. Sam couldn't feel anything, but he blamed everything that went wrong in his life on not having a father. His father had died when he was only five and he had worked all his life to distance himself from those feelings. Cognitively, Sam knew that *everything* bad couldn't possibly be the fault of growing up without a father, but that's how he felt. He blamed his inability to have friends, his emotional distance from women, his lack of ability to make and keep money, his insomnia, his lack of purpose in life, his lack of talent in sports, his being uncomfortable around authority figures, and more, all on this one issue.

Because he reported that he had no feelings, Karin started with a different technique. She said, "Sam, you know that little boy inside you better than anyone in the world. What *would* he be feeling in this situation? What do you *imagine* he is feeling?" Karin had Sam make up a story about how that little 5 year old would feel, and using the Movie Technique, they tapped for all the feelings and aspects that Sam guessed that five year old would be feeling. As they tapped, Sam's eyes got a bit watery, but he continued to report he felt nothing.

As they finished the session, Sam said, "Even though, it seems to me that I wasn't feeling anything, the belief I had seems to have changed anyway. I know my father died and it was terrible to grow up without a father, but now it seems silly to blame everything on it. It's like I *knew* it before now, but I just didn't *feel* it. And now I'm kind of embarrassed that I blamed everything on it. I mean, other children lose their father and they don't blame everything on it."Karin then suggested that Sam tap for the embarrassment he now felt.

Whenever you work with low intensity of feelings that can't be articulated, remember the power of being as specific as possible. Another technique that can help you get specific is focusing on memories.

"What memory do you have that you would rather not have?" Tap for all the aspects of that memory, tap for all parts. Tap with all the points, no short cuts. These clients may signal they are finished by changing the subject. At the next session, ask again what memory they would particularly like to do without. It usually turns out to be a different memory.

Pick a picture. Another helpful way to deal with little or no emotion is to use submodalities. For example, EFT Master Gwyneth Moss asks clients, "What one picture represents the worst of the event? Can you give the picture a name?" Help clients describe this picture using submodalities by asking, "Is it close to you or distant? Is it bright or dull? Is it in black and white or in color? Is it 3D or flat? What else do you notice about it?" Tap for all aspects in the picture, then check to see if the qualities of the picture have changed.

Some clients bury their emotions about an issue in a negative self-belief. Address this possibility by asking, "What do you think about yourself when you recall that picture?" Have the client state the negative belief, measure its "truth" (VOC is useful here), then tap for the picture.

Ask for a drawing. Having the client draw a picture of the issue allows you and the client to "see the whole picture" and gives the client a concrete focus. Even if the image is abstract, you can tap about the elements in the picture, the colors, qualities of line, and so on.

Pretend. If your client can remember an event but has no emotion around it, have her make up the emotion. Clients know the person in the event (themselves) better than anyone else. Ask: "*If* that person had an emotion about this event, what would the emotion be? Make it up or guess." Then continue as though the emotion were real.

Being Gentle with Yourself

For some people, just considering thinking about traumatic events can cause such strong emotional reactions that they can't even get started. You've learned many concepts that you can use to help clients who aren't ready to deal with their own issues, but if this happens while doing your own work, it can be very unnerving. Usually, the best course of action is just *tap anyway*. This can be a great opportunity to resolve issues that come up for you, even if that issue is that you don't want to think about resolving the issue.

If after tapping, you feel worse, however, you may be working on issues that are very complex and would be difficult for anyone to handle alone. Don't get discouraged. Persistence is often called for in complex issues – and we all have some complex issues. You might tap for "Even though it seems tapping is making me feel worse, I deeply and completely accept myself anyway. Even though it seems tapping is not working for me, I appreciate my courage in beginning to look at my issues. Even though my body feels _____, I deeply and completely accept that I am doing the best I can."

If tapping doesn't reduce the intensity or brings up further upsetting details that upset you even more and continuing to tap doesn't help, stop – take a break, go take a walk, do something physically active. You may be trying to do too much too soon. But don't give up. It can be very difficult to find and resolve our deepest core issues by ourselves. You may be able to chop off the top of the weeds in your garden but unable to get to the roots. Therefore, it may appear EFT is not working or it may even feel that tapping makes you feel worse. Call a tapping buddy or make an appointment with an experienced practitioner. Even the most experienced EFT practitioners sometimes need the help of other practitioners.

Test Your Knowledge

1. True or false? In order to work effectively with a client's issue, you need to know the specific details of the issue.

2. All of the following statements are true of the Tearless Trauma Technique except
a. The client should remain dissociated from the details of the event.
b. The client should guess at all intensity levels.
c. By definition, the technique is always tearless.
d. The client should be encouraged to focus on vague terms instead of specifics.

3. True or false? When a client complains of a physical issue, you should recommend that a physician be consulted.

4. True or false? When pain doesn't decrease and just moves to a different location in the body, EFT is not working.

5. Which technique begins with guessing what the intensity would be if the issue were to be the focus?
a. Tearless Trauma
b. Sneaking Up on the Problem
c. Chasing the Pain

6. Which option _best_ defines Sneaking up?
a. Sneaking up addresses their fear without dealing with it directly.
b. Sneaking up is a method used by practitioners to dig deeper.
c. Sneaking up is best used on traumas that involved sneaky behavior.

7. When using the Tearless Trauma Technique you tap before you go directly to the event until the intensity is guessed to be
a. 7 – 10
b. 6 – 4
c. 3 – 0

8. True or false? When emotional intensity is high, the client is ready for a breakthrough, so it's important to push on to resolution.

Answers can be found in Appendix E

Chapter 4 – Leaving the Dungeon

Watch the Movie Technique

Creating a movie of the event pretty much guarantees you are dealing with a specific event, which is important to your successful use of EFT. Generally, to use this technique, you begin by asking the client a series of questions.

Could you make a short movie of this event? Remember that at no point in this movie is it necessary for clients to tell *you* the details. The critical part is that *they* are tuned in with all five senses. Ask them to focus on what they see, hear, feel, smell, taste. Caveat: If they become immediately upset when just beginning to think about the movie, start tapping without asking them to focus on the situation more closely. If they are very upset, use a distancing technique. Tap until they are calm enough to be more specific.

How long would your movie last? You want to make sure it is a short movie, three minutes or less. Often the key traumatic event in a movie is only seconds long. Help your client break the movie down into as many small pieces as necessary to address each specific upsetting event.

What would the title be? Help the client identify a name that is specific to that movie. If the movie chosen was about the time when his brother scared him so badly he wet his pants in front of the other boys, who then made fun of him, the name of the movie could be something like "Wet my pants," "Brother scared me," or "The boys laughed." The point is to have the client focus on one important aspect of the movie as he taps. *Note:* Depending on the client's willingness to address the movie directly, sometimes making the title *less* specific may be easier for the client. For example, "That terrible night" rather than "The night I caught my husband cheating."

Use the client's movie title and tap. For example: "Even though I have this [title] movie, I fully and totally accept myself anyway." And use a Reminder Phrase with the title of the movie, "This [title] movie." If the intensity is high, tap several sequences until the client reports that the intensity is down to at least mid-range. If the emotion is very intense, you may choose to back up and tap more generally about fears of addressing the movie before getting more specific.

Run the movie. Ask the client: "When you run the movie in your mind, what is the intensity level?" Note that the movie can first be run silently. Continue to tap for other parts or aspects of the movie. The client may choose to change the title of the movie as the tapping progresses. After he reports the intensity as 3 or below, ask if he is willing to talk about the incident. While he doesn't *have* to talk about it, telling the story of the event can help bring up other unresolved aspects. If he does not want to talk about it, work to help him look at all the details using questions that address submodalities.

Would you be willing to tell me about the movie now? If he does tell you, be sure you stop at any point that is upsetting, even a little bit. Tap at any point of intensity until that part is down to 0, and then continue the narration of the movie. If he is hesitant to tell you any details, you could ask him to imagine the details and tap while imagining them. This process both helps reduce intensity and starts to clear any shame or embarrassment about the event.

Now rerun the movie in its entirety again. Address *any* intensity to *any* part of the movie. Make sure the *entire movie* is clear before you move on.

Medium and Low Intensity with the Movie Technique

In the last section, we discussed being prepared for high intensity and abreactions. When using the Movie Technique, if a client goes into very high intensity, assure him he is safe now with you. Ask him to put the movie across the street, in a box, behind a curtain, or use some other distancing concept. Remember that you can tap without words, because the fact that there is obvious emotion means the client is already tuned in. If the client is ready to tap, but not to talk about specifics, you can tap for a vague statement (but still specific to the person) like "Even though I have this upsetting movie... Even though it scares me to think about that movie behind the screen... Even though I have this [title] movie and I wish I didn't..."

A mid-range intensity is ideal for the Movie Technique and other standard EFT techniques where distancing is not required. This range has sufficient intensity to measure results, but not so much as to cause the person significant emotional pain.

Sometimes you will be dealing with very low intensity. Some clients will come to you with stress-related symptoms but will tell you about traumatic events with little or no emotion. These people are already quite adept at distancing or dissociation. They will often not even realize that they still feel strongly about an event and yet they somehow feel its effects. These clients are actually more challenging to work with than clients presenting with high intensity because their low affect makes it very difficult to test the effects of tapping. It may even be difficult, at first, to find an issue with enough reaction to create a tapping sequence. When someone presents with little or no affect, try using the Movie Technique emphasizing the five senses. Work to help the client *intensify* all the submodalities around the movie, especially focusing on sensations in the body that these memories bring up. Clients who have learned to bury emotions may find it much easier to begin by identifying the queasy stomach or lump in the throat that the memory engenders. If successful, this will raise the intensity enough to move into the Movie Technique itself. And, as suggested previously, ask clients to tell you how they know they don't feel anything. You can create Setups from identifying how much they are *not* feeling.

The Difference Between the Movie and Tearless Trauma Techniques

You learned about using the Tearless Trauma Technique in level 1 and learned here how Craig used it with groups. You learned that when using Tearless Trauma, clients guess what their intensity rating would be *if* they were to look at their issue, and that this is a helpful technique when you believe that having the client go directly to the specifics of the issue would create very high intensity.

A movie scene of an event is *specific*. The movie begins at a specific point in time; it has specific scenes and characters. But is that the only difference between

Tearless Trauma and the Movie Technique? The following chart details the differences, step by step, between these two useful techniques.

Movie Technique	Tearless Trauma Technique
Dissociates client from event.	*Doubly* dissociates client from event.
Is used when client is willing and able to look at event, so begins by practitioner asking movie questions.	Is used when client finds thinking about looking at event too upsetting to go there yet.
Is used when event is talked about specifically.	Is used when event is stated in *vague* terms.
Reviews movie for length.	Does not address length.
Gives event a specific name, such as *Johnny hit me*, to use as a Reminder Phrase.	Uses very vague wording for a Reminder Phrase. *This scary event the time I was 10...*
Assesses the intensity of the event	*Guesses* the intensity *if* event were looked at.
Taps on event until intensity is 3 or below.	Taps until intensity is *guessed* to be at 3 or below.
Asks client to vividly imagine the movie. Helps client get specific using all five senses: *what was seen, heard, felt, smelled, or tasted.*	At 3 or below, helps client begin to look at issue in small segments.
Asks client to imagine the movie in detail and give practitioner an intensity level. Keeps tapping until intensity is 3 or below.	Continues tapping until the intensity for each segment is 0.
Asks client to narrate the movie.	Asks client to tell the story out loud.
Stops at any intensity and taps until 0.	Stops at any intensity and taps until 0. If, at any point, client becomes very upset, instructs the client to *stop* focusing on it. Suggests distancing technique, e.g., putting it behind a wall. Goes back to *guessing*.
Continues tapping until the client can narrate the entire movie without emotion.	Has client repeat the story and checks for any remaining intensity until 0 on all parts.

Tell the Story Technique

This technique can be used in conjunction with the Movie Technique or can stand on its own. *Your client simply tells you about the event starting before the event occurred*. You stop at any point of intensity to deal with the intensity and related aspects. Tap until the client is calm about that part or aspect *before* going on with the story. Ask questions for clarification, if necessary, but *do not make interpretations*. When you have tapped through the entire story, test by having the client tell you the entire story again calmly. One way to test whether the emotional impact of the story is resolved is to notice if the client can tell you the story in far more detail. Review Gary Craig's suggestions from his manual or find more information in *The EFT Level 1 Comprehensive Training Resource* if necessary.

Submodalities for Specificity

Now that the client is able to address the issue with the Watch the Movie or Tell the Story Technique, making use of submodalities can help to make descriptions more specific. They can be used as metaphors for memory, pain, or other physical feelings. In addition, they can be used after tapping to help test progress.

As your client tells her story or describes her movie, help her notice and define the relevant submodalities in order to get more specific. Ask questions that would help the client describe what she is seeing, hearing, feeling, tasting, or smelling. The most traumatic part of the memory might be a sound (like the screaming) or a smell (like the burning) rather than what was actually seen. Never assume it's the sight that triggers the negative memory. It could be any submodality or a combination of them.

As the tapping for emotions and aspects balances the energy around a memory, it can begin to look, sound, feel, taste, and smell different. The client may first describe the memory as bright and vivid, close and noisy, but then, as she becomes calmer, she could state that the picture of the memory has become much smaller, dimmer, and farther away. Using the reported submodalities, we can determine our progress through the client's report of changes in those submodalities.

Use questions about all five senses to help uncover submodalities.

Visual: Is it close or far away? Clear or foggy? What color is it? Is it big or small? Is it just one image or lots of images? Is it flat or in 3D? What shape is it? Does it look like real life or is it more like a flat poster? Does it move around or is it still?

Auditory: What direction does it come from? Is it loud or low? Does the sound move around? Is there one voice or many? What is being said? What do you hear in the background?

Kinesthetic: Does it have a size? A texture? Rough or smooth? Hard or soft? Is there pressure? What is the temperature? Cool or hot sensation? Where is it located in the body? Is it moving around or still?

Olfactory/Gustatory: What does it taste like? What does it smell like? Is it sweet or sour? Salty? Bitter? How would you define the smell?

Role-Play for Specificity or Testing

Role-playing an event can be used to help clients get to the most intense part of a story. The practitioner and/or the client can role-play the event or the person that is part of the problem in the client's life. It can also be used after tapping to 0 as an excellent way to test the results of EFT and uncover any missed aspects whenever another person triggered the client. Ask the client to play the person involved and to show you what the person did that triggered a response. One of Gary's methods in such cases was to ask his client to "Teach me how to do that." However you set up the role-play, whether you reenact the scene or mimic the person's behavior, whether you have your client act or you both take a role, the goal is to make the role-play as realistic as you can. Help the client to notice the person's tone, posture, gestures, and the look in their eyes. Where were they sitting or standing in the room? Who else was there? Was there anything else in the environment that impacted the event? Use this method to uncover and address all the aspects you can.

 ## Test Your Knowledge

1. True or false? The first step when using the Movie Technique is to instruct clients to run through the entire movie in their minds.

2. All of the following are true of the Movie Technique except:
a. The Movie Technique should be applied to a specific event.
b. The movie should always be three minutes or less.
c. When testing, the client should rerun the entire movie, and when done, all moments in the movie that continue to carry intensity should be addressed at once.
d. The client does not need to relate the events of the movie out loud until he is ready.

3. True or false? The Tell the Story Technique can be used effectively along with the Watch the Movie Technique, or by itself.

4. True or false? When using the Tell the Story Technique, the client only has to tell the story once.

Answers can be found in Appendix E

Opening the Doors to the Palace

Gary Craig expounds on his metaphor of the Palace of Possibilities in the writings and DVD sets in which he discussed using EFT to achieve one's full potential (Craig, nda). In these articles and videos, he explains that we all live in palaces with many beautiful rooms, all open to us, all full of unlimited possibilities, but the walls are covered with writing. The writings tell us who we are and what we are allowed to do. Many of us see "keep out" signs all around our "palaces" and so we stay in just a few spare or familiar rooms never venturing where we "don't belong" because we obey the writing on our walls without question.

Chapter 5 – The Writing on the Walls

The English idiom "the writing on the wall" refers to the ultimate limit, the end. Craig uses this metaphor to refer to the limiting beliefs we all have. He describes the writing on the walls of our palaces as our *core beliefs,* our "truth," or "the way things are," which can be both positive and negative. At times, the writings on our walls guide us and keep us safe. At other times, they keep us from reaching our full potential. The writing is generally put there by those we've accepted as the authorities in our lives: parents, teachers, religious leaders, even peers and TV.

Often, the writing is our interpretation of an event. Many times the writing is from what others said to us (or something we overheard). Sometimes it was said just once, but often it was said to us repeatedly. The writing on our walls can state positive things about us and the world or negative things about us and the world.

This writing is not always put there by words. You also interpret others' facial expressions, gestures, and movements such as rolling of the eyes, turning away when you speak, sighing, subtle headshakes, and frowns. Such physiological expressions by others can write just as heavily on your walls. You will hear many times that the way clients interpreted a "look" from a parent is imprinted on their walls just as strongly as though it was said to them.

Some of this writing gives us important guidelines or rules that are useful and helpful like "look both ways before crossing the street." Often, however, the writing is negative and limiting. You might think we would resent limitations or, once we grow up, toss them aside. Remember, though, that what is firmly written on our walls is the truth to us; it becomes our interpretation of the world. Even though it limits our potential, everything we do is an attempt to validate or satisfy this "truth," whether the net result is positive or negative. Since we believe it to be the truth, validating it is simply how we make sense of things.

Craig (nda) explains it this way, "There is an old saying that goes, 'Nothing has any meaning except the meaning we give it.' I have found it quite useful over the years but wish to restate it now to fit within the Palace of Possibilities metaphor. Restated, it goes like this, 'Nothing has any meaning except that which is written on our walls'" (p. 137). In other words, the writing on our walls is how we understand the world around us and our place in it.

Every interpretation, every decision we make about life is made by consulting this writing on our walls. The writing contains the shoulds, should nots, cans, and cannots that determine what we believe we are capable of, how the world works, and what is true of ourselves and other people.

You may have writing like this on your walls:
- *Men always…*
- *Women never…*
- *All people of the ___ race are greedy.*
- *All people of the ___ race are smart.*
- *I'm ugly.*
- *You're beautiful.*
- *Keep your looks whatever it costs.*

- *People who worry about looks are shallow.*
- *Making a lot of money makes you successful.*
- *Caring about money is selfish.*
- *Policemen are your friend.*
- *Policemen are corrupt and will try to frame you.*
- *Chevys are the best cars.*
- *Fords are the best cars.*
- *Mental problems run in our family so of course you have problems.*
- *No one in our family has mental problems.*
- *You'll never amount to anything.*
- *You can be anything you want.*
- *You're nothing.*
- *You're special.*

We have many, many writings – every belief addressing every area of our perceptions about ourselves and the world is found on our walls. "We constantly consult the writing on our walls to make meaning of the things we see, hear, feel, etc." (Craig, nda, p. 139). We have a need to make sense of the world around us and we always try to do it in a manner that fits our existing beliefs, that is, matches the writing on our walls.

Understanding that the writing on the walls is truth for us helps us understand how we hang on to the attitudes, opinion, and beliefs that make up our values, judgments, and behaviors, and how these, in turn, affect our perceptions and how we view the world. We all have this writing, but because, for instance, I believe *my* writing is true, I can't see any errors in it. I can, however, see the errors on *your* walls. It's important for everyone, but especially for practitioners, to realize that disagreements with others are caused by the writing on *our* walls not matching the writing on *their* walls.

Understanding this concept is helpful in accepting people and accepting people *where they are;* this is a key concept in counseling. Accepting people where they are can be difficult when we are busy consulting the writing on our own walls even as we are trying to help others. For this reason, as practitioners, it's imperative that we commit to "do our own work," to resolve as many of our own issues as we can. Because we can't see our own limits and errors, it is often necessary for us to have assistance from someone else. Fortunately, our own limiting beliefs, reinforced by the writing on our walls, can be changed using EFT.

So how do we change these writings? The writings are so extensive that we must categorize and organize them. If something new happens, we will try to fit the new event into an existing category and, in this way, when we are able to lump new information in with the old, our writing is validated and reinforced.

Swiss developmental psychologist Jean Piaget (1896–1980) first espoused the concept that people deal with new information in one of two ways. The first, and by far most preferable to the majority of people, is to *assimilate* the new into the familiar (Penrose, 1979). This explains why we are constantly validating our "truth."

Piaget described the only other option for taking in new information: *accommodation*. By this he meant that we must *accommodate* the information by *creating a new system* in our heads, thus *changing* our existing beliefs (Penrose, 1979). Accommodating the new information in this way actually requires a paradigm shift, a change in belief, a change in the writing on our walls.

Since accommodating new information is more difficult, it's fortunate that EFT can help to effect that change. Where the writings on our walls are negative for us, we can, with the help of EFT, change them, thus neutralizing their life-limiting effects. One EFTer described the change saying that using EFT for the writing on his walls was like checking through a list on a dry erase board. EFT helped him "erase" all the negative learning on that board, one line at a time.

Craig described accommodation as "filling in the blanks." When a new experience presents itself that *isn't* written on our walls, *and* we can't fit that experience into some similar writing that *is* there, we fill in the blanks as best we can. In fact, Craig states that the point at which a client begins to "fill in the blank" is the point at which EFT effects a real change. "In some cases, listening to the changes in how clients fill in the blanks can be more useful than the 0-10 scale because it often points to more global healing. The 0-10 scale is quite useful, of course, but nothing is as useful as the cognition change that is evidenced by how the client fills in the blanks. That cognition change is the true bottom line." (Craig, nda, p. 138)

Supporting the Cognitive Shift

For many, the term "cognitive shift" implies a change in thinking. As EFT Master Barbara Smith (2007) states in her article "Cognitive Shifts That Work," the term "cognitive shift" has been used "in psychiatry, mostly it seems, to describe the kind of downward slide in perception and behavior made by some psychiatric patients when they shift in and out of various types of psychotic states. In the dictionary, most definitions of cognition include *knowing, perceiving, and awareness, as well as thinking, reasoning, and understanding.* Inherent in this definition are the concepts of the conscious mind, the subconscious mind, and unconscious process."

In EFT, we see a cognitive shift as more than just a change in thinking or intention; we see that it involves change in all layers of consciousness – a realization or change in perspective or belief.

Smith continues, "When we are working with EFT, we engage our everyday knowing, thinking and understanding, and at the same time we access deeper levels of consciousness, usually expressed through the body, as we physically tap into our energy system. Using the tapping sequence to access these deeper levels is often the difference that makes a difference."

As you strive to "make a difference," listen for the cognitive shift where the client reports that in some way the issue is over, that the client has survived, learned from it, and is ready to move on. One of the most interesting parts of conducting EFT sessions is watching the cognitive shifts – the changes in perception and beliefs that occur naturally as the client resolves the issues. Listen closely and clients will tell you the writing on their walls. As tapping resolves an issue, they erase the existing writing or reword it to represent a different and more positive interpretation. That different interpretation, or cognitive change, is what represents true change and resolution. We might even equate Piaget's term of *accommodation* with our palace. When we must *provide accommodations* for a new and more positive belief, we may welcome that new idea, not just by erasing the writing about it, but by tossing that old "keep out" sign and throwing open the doors to a whole new beautiful room in the palace!

 Test Your Knowledge

1. True or false? All of the "writing on our walls" is negative and limiting.

2. True or false? We most often try to find a way to fit new experiences in to the "truth" that we already know.

3. True or false? The "writing on our walls" can be the result of something said to us, implied, or overheard.

4. True or false? Practitioners need to be aware of the "writing" on their own walls unless they are using gentle techniques where they don't need to know the details of their clients' issues.

5. All of the below are true, except
a. Our perception of ourselves and the world is influenced by what our parents said and did as we grew up.
b. The "writings on our walls" affect how we interpret what other people are saying.
c. We can use EFT to change perception, and, therefore, change our reality.
d. We cannot change the learning of our past; we need just to get over it.

Answers can be found in Appendix E

Chapter 6 – Reading the Writing

So you've trashed the "keep out" sign and thrown open the door... Okay, maybe you've gently set aside the "keep out" sign and cracked open the door enough to peek out.... How *exactly* do you change what you *know* is "the truth"? How can you help someone else change his or her "truth"? How can we all leave behind the familiar rooms in which we feel safe, to freely explore the marvelous potential of the palace?

Getting to the Core Issue

The key is in identifying which of the writings on your walls is holding the presenting problem in place. Recall from level 1 that the presenting problem, the problem the client comes in with, often the thing that is interfering with the client's life in some way, can be like a puzzle. Each piece may have many sides or *aspects*, and you need to tap on one specific piece at a time.

> Some pieces are more critical to completing the puzzle. These are often the *core issues* [emphasis added] behind your presenting problem that must be addressed to solve the problem... When putting a puzzle together, sometimes it seems you search and search to find a particular piece. When you do find that elusive piece, it then seems that other pieces now easily fit into place. Dealing with our issues can be similar: we get one piece here and one piece there and finally we find our *core issue*; then many of other related little pieces no longer seem so formidable. They were "put into place" when you found the *core issue*. (Adams & Davidson, 2011)

The "core issue" is the basic negative belief, written on the walls of our palace, that maintains the problem. Recall that Freud established that our minds actually maintain and support our issues. Ann discusses this in her EFT4PowerPoint Training Package: "The prevailing idea, until Freud, was that healing psychological/emotional trauma was just a matter of wanting to change or exhibiting enough willpower to 'get over it.' Freud introduced the idea that the brain itself... actually works to maintain emotional issues...so that it would take more than just willpower to fix it...Craig, like Freud, realized it took more than willpower to resolve emotional suffering. EFT is one of the techniques that gives sufferers of psychological and emotional trauma more than just willpower to work with." (Adams, 2011a)

Core issues hold our problems in place even if we work out some of the presenting problems they cause; they are the foundation that supports all the related issues. Until the core issue is addressed, the problem will not be totally resolved.

In level 1, you learned yet another way of thinking of this concept, that of "Peeling the Onion." You practiced identifying aspects and reinforced the need always to be specific and to deal with each aspect separately. In level 1, you focused on the way an issue could shift aspects. For example, if you were passed over for a promotion, you might start out feeling angry that your boss didn't appreciate your work or that a coworker sabotaged your chance for promotion. You might then move to the guilt that you felt when you told your spouse you didn't get the promotion, moving then to your spouse's reaction to the news, and then to shame that your friends would think you weren't "good enough." (Adams & Davidson, 2011)

In level 2, you will focus on finding that deeper negative belief written on your walls. This is the belief that causes you to feel more than the understandable disappointment at not getting a promotion. It's the "core issue" that leaves you feeling, rather, that this isn't just a temporary setback or a disappointing turn of events or something that *happened to you,* but that it actually has something to do with *who you are.*

This is the type of assimilation that we do that causes emotional baggage. If we have "I'll never accomplish anything" on our walls, and in our need to validate that, interpret this event to fit the writing, we may come up with something that says, "I didn't get the promotion, I'll never get it, I'll never accomplish anything." If we don't consciously recognize that we are dealing with the core issue of fearing that we'll never be able to succeed, the issue may manifest in headaches, overeating, fighting with a spouse, reckless driving – who knows?

Imagine a client comes to you, saying, "I can't stop eating sweets. I've gained fifty pounds since I was passed over for a promotion, but that was no big deal." You won't know it until you find the core issue, but what really needs to change is not his diet, but his belief that he'll never succeed in life.

Another metaphor that can be helpful to understanding and visualizing the relationship between aspects and core issues is that of the Tabletop.

Tabletops

When clients come for help, they often give general descriptions of their problems. The Tabletop metaphor is useful for getting to the specifics and core beliefs that support presenting problems.

The metaphor of a table is similar to the "Peeling the Onion" metaphor in that the top of the table is seen as the "core" and may have many legs (layers). In the EFT Intermediate Library, "Tutorial #5: Anatomy of an Emotional Issue," the writing on the walls was equated with the top of the table. The beauty of the Tabletop metaphor is that a "core issue" or belief must have experiences to support it, to hold it up. The metaphor helps us visualize the specifics that prove the belief or make it real to us as the "legs" holding up the belief or problem. The specific legs can be anything from a feeling in the pit of the stomach to the memory of something someone said. The value of the Tabletop metaphor is that it helps us focus on and tap on those specifics.

This is a useful metaphor for demonstrating why issues can be very complex. You can seem to be making progress, and then progress slows or stops. You seem to have only partial results, or you get relief, then your problem seems to come back. In times like this, the Tabletop metaphor can be extended to one of tables stacked on top of other tables. The leg (aspect) of one table might be stacked on top of another table so that the leg, itself, becomes its own tabletop. In order to find the "proof" that supports this one leg, we need to get even more specific, identifying the legs that support that leg (now its own tabletop).

Craig often described addressing and resolving issues as "collapsing" them. The Tabletop metaphor is useful in imagining, for instance, the legs of one table collapsing leaving only Tabletops (core beliefs) atop one another. For example, if the presenting problem is that the client is unhappy in her marriage, it may be revealed, that this issue (tabletop) stands on top of many other tables. Several underlying tabletops may need to collapse before the major tabletop is finally able to fall.

Ann discusses the relationship between the Tabletop metaphor and another metaphor, the Forest, in her EFT4PowerPoint Training Package:

> The EFT Intermediate Library "Tutorial #5: Anatomy of an Emotional Issue" also drew parallels between the metaphor of the tabletop and the forest. It was said prior to Tutorial #5 that the forest represented global issues and that, sometimes, if one or two trees were cut, the whole "forest would fall," illustrating *generalization*. Tutorial #5 sought to replace the forest metaphor with the tabletop. As always, you should use the metaphors that suit your style and help your clients and trainees understand the concepts. [One] interpretation of the diseased forest metaphor for generalization is that a diseased forest falling is something you notice when it happens, something of a happy accident. Like generalization, it's not something you can "force" to happen or consciously create. It happens from the top down with the large issue falling on the small specific ones. The concept of the Tabletop, on the other hand, is a concept you can use from the bottom up to help you get even more specific in identifying the incidents and feelings that support your larger issue. (Adams, 2011b)

You will need to tap for all aspects around each specific event (leg) under each tabletop. It is possible that the legs of the tabletop you are working on are also being held up by one or more other tabletops. All legs of these additional tabletops must be addressed before the issue is completely resolved. In short, sometimes your problem cannot disappear entirely until you discover and deal with all underlying tabletops.

Some table legs are shared. In *EFT Level 1 Comprehensive Training Resource*, it was discussed that many events function as a reconfirmation of a core belief.

There can be events and negative learnings that are legs on two different tables at the same time, so we use EFT to resolve legs, one at a time, to get to and clear the core event of each issue. It is often important to explain this concept to clients so they don't give up on using EFT. Few issues are "one-minute wonders." It may take time and persistence to clear negative beliefs that are attached to each other or stacked on top of each other. One of the most useful tools the practitioner has for helping the client access these beliefs is skillful questioning.

Asking Questions

Although the core issue, or driving influence, behind a problem is sometimes right out in front, good questioning is generally necessary to uncover core issues that keep a longstanding problem or a pattern of problems in place.

Asking your client questions helps in finding aspects and uncovering core issues. There may be many aspects. It may seem as if you have addressed all the aspects when another one pops up. It may seem that even the core issues have aspects and core issues of their own. Sometimes the process of looking for a core issue leads in multiple directions. Some of these directions may lead away from the core issue. Finding the core issue(s) is part of the real artistry and mastery of EFT and a central focus at level 2.

As you begin working with others, always begin by encouraging clients to tell you of *anything* that comes up as they tap – anything – new thoughts, pictures, or images. These spontaneous insights are often very useful. Don't dismiss *anything* as being unrelated or uninvolved. Anything the client brings up is relevant. It's all connected.

One of Gary Craig's examples of a hard-to-find core issue was the story of Nate and his fear of heights (Craig, ndb, p. 18). Nate said the fear developed after a parachute jump from a helicopter. Nate was not making much headway in eradicating his fear of heights until he discovered his core issue was the sense of ridicule he felt when he had been teased and prodded to make a parachute jump from a helicopter. When the sense of ridicule was resolved, the fear of heights vanished.

We don't know much more than that about the real Nate, but we can use this example to explore the way core issues can lead to more than one problem. Since soldiers ribbing one another is a normal part of the military experience, it makes one wonder if Nate's emotional response about being ridiculed started at the parachute jump. It's possible, but it seems more likely that Nate's issue would have started much earlier. Could collapsing the event of the ridicule about parachuting have been enough to collapse his response to all other ridicule events in his life? Perhaps. Although addressing the parachute ridicule was sufficient to eliminate the fear of heights, for our hypothetical Nate, we would notice that Nate's reaction to ridicule was disproportionately strong. He had severely limited his life, avoiding all heights in reaction to this event, so we might explore the possibility that Nate may continue to limit his life or react inappropriately to anything he interprets as ridicule. This possibility was not brought up or tested in the original story. The real Nate was satisfied to work on his fear of heights. He stopped there. Going on or stopping is always the client's choice.

In longer sessions and over a period of time, if Nate were our client, it might be helpful to explore other times and ways that Nate felt ridiculed. Since his reaction to ridicule was so powerful, finding other ridicule events and testing to ensure that these experiences were also neutralized could be important for future reactions to anything he might interpret similarly. Could he be free from a fear of heights *and* be able to respond to any future ridicule in a calm, rational manner? Quite possibly. Not that Nate would ever like being ridiculed (no one *likes* ridicule) – it would still be annoying. But if the issue were truly resolved, Nate would see it as the other person's problem, and not interpret it to mean there was something wrong with him. Remember, the negative beliefs that tend to affect us most are the ones that seem to say something, not just about what happened to us, but about who we are.

If Nate still had problems with ridicule, but seemed to have blocked out the core issue or to be too afraid to "go there," you could, of course, use Sneaking Up on the core issue or one of the other Gentle Techniques, but if Nate were ready to go further, but didn't yet have a specific detail or event to work on, you could begin with relevant detective questions: who, what, when, where, why, how. You would keep asking until you and Nate reached some specific to work with.

Questions are the most effective tool for gathering the information you need to help clients develop specific Setups and to find core issues. When a client comes in with a general description of the problem, such as "I don't like my job," getting to the *real* issue, "I don't fit in," can take some detective work. Questions can lead to a tappable issue, which can then lead to an even deeper core issue, "I'm unlovable."

There is an infinite variety of questions that can help a client get deeper into the issue or clarify a specific event. Review questions in *EFT Level 1 Comprehensive Training Resource* for more variations on types of questions such as these:

- *How do you feel about having this problem?*
- *How do you know you have this problem?*
- *When did you feel like this before?*
- *What do you feel this is all about?*
- *When was the first time you remember feeling this way?*
- *What does this issue or person remind you of?*
- *And that is like...? And that is like...?*
- *If there were an event related to this one, what would it be?*
- *If you could live your life over again, what person or event would you prefer to skip?*
- *Can you be more specific as to what exactly you are depressed/anxious/ angry/ etc. about?*
- *How will you know when you are no longer depressed/anxious/angry/etc.?*
- *If you had a boat with all the events in your life in it and the boat began to sink, what event(s) would you toss over first?*
- *If there were an emotional component or contributor to this problem, what would it be?*

Ideas for more questions come, in part, from EFT Master Lindsay Kenny (2008):

- *If this illness/pain or body part had a voice, what would it say?*
- *What was going on in your life around the time this problem started?*
- *When did it start? (Many times clients need to talk generally about their lives pre-pain before the pain before they remember anything related to their physical problem.)*
- *What would you lose or give up in your life if you got over this illness/pain?*
- *What is this pain holding you back from accomplishing?*
- *How do you feel about having this symptom or pain?*
- *How do you benefit from this illness/pain?*
- *What do you feel angriest about?*
- *Why might you deserve this?*
- *Which emotions are most current for you now? What other situations in your life hold those same emotions? What are the stressors behind those emotions?*
- *Is there a relationship between stress in your life and your pain?*
- *What is a metaphor for this pain/symptom that applies to your life?*

Tapping then brings up other aspects or issues, and often the need for more questions before further tapping. As you find the issues, continue to refine the questions to make them more and more relevant to the specific problem. When one event is resolved, you want to know if there are other similar events that could be affecting the core issue. A perfect question at the end of each round to check for additional aspects is, "What comes up for you now?"

What Comes Up for You Now?

"What comes up for you now?" is a valuable question when you are working to find core events. Anything that comes up is linked to the issue at hand. Is there some movement or change, or a spontaneous thought, sensation, a new memory of a different event, a fresh emotional reaction, a belief about the event or people involved? Help the client figure out how the new finding is tied into or linked to the presenting issue.

In response to this question, people tend to give a response that is event-related, emotion-related, sensation-related, or belief-related.

Event-Related

The client may bring up the memory of another specific event that is related to the original event or he may bring up another event that is, in some way, like the event he is addressing. For example, as a client works on issues around his recent car accident, he may remember another accident he had at age sixteen, then a near accident with his mother when he was eight, then an accident when he was younger and asleep in the backseat where he awoke from landing on the floor and an ambulance came and took his father to the hospital.

Emotion-Related

The client may trace her dominant emotional reaction back to events that generated similar emotions. Easily feeling embarrassed today could link back to being embarrassed as a child, for example, by the church choir director.

The client may bring up a similar emotion related to the situation or to a person involved in the event. Intense events that caused a strong emotional reaction in a child can lead to the child associating that same strong emotion with the participant or perpetrator even in other situations. For example, feeling frustration at having to care for an aged parent might be linked to the frustration the client felt as a child having been left waiting outside a bar for that same parent.

Sensation-Related

Strong sensory stimuli often link to emotionally charged events. Pay close attention when clients describe sights, sounds, textures, tastes, and smells. For example, John felt sick to his stomach every time he smelled the smoke from his neighbors outside grilling. John traced the feeling back to the time when he was four, when he'd played with the squirrels in his backyard, chasing them around, leaving treats, watching them run scrambling into the trees. One day his father shot two of the squirrels, skinned, and grilled them. John was terrified and devastated to have lost his playmates and the smell of them cooking had made him sick.

Remember to use the client's awareness of physical sensations to help uncover emotional response. Ask, "Does any other physical sensation come up?

71

What does that sensation link to? Where do you feel this upset in your body?" Setups can focus on the physical response. Often, when the physical response is clear, the issue either becomes clearer or is resolved. When testing to assess the level of completion, ask clients to go inside and scan their body for any remaining physical reaction. "Now, close your eyes and scan your body. Is the feeling you described earlier still there? Has it changed in any way?"

Belief-Related

Asking what comes up will also, at times, lead to a response regarding negative or limiting beliefs. When intense events happen, they often lead to a decision about ourselves and our place in the world that we write on our walls. As a result, we can sometimes remember what we decided during the event that is still affecting us so strongly. If clients bring up a belief, you can combine it with an awareness of their physical response to it. Ask the client to say the limiting belief out loud and ask what the physical response is to the statement.

As you think about related events, remember the generalization effect. We may not have to tap on every single related event for the entire core issue to be resolved. (Refer to *EFT Level 1 Comprehensive Training Resource* to review this concept.)

 Test Your Knowledge

1. True or false? Often, you will work on several minor issues or events before finding the core issue.

2. Which of the following statements is true?
a. It is unacceptable to ask your client to make up a story about an event or issue if the client doesn't know the core issue.
b. It's important that clients know what's bothering them before tapping.
c. As you tap with highly charged aspects, other previously unfelt aspects surface.
d. None of the above.

3. True or false? You should help the client dismiss irrelevant details that come up so that you can continue looking for the core issue.

Answers can be found in Appendix E

Chapter 7 – Erasing the Writing

Using Setups

As we identify issues, often through questioning, we use what we've learned to develop specific Setups. A Setup is intended to *state either a specific issue or a specific time when* a disturbing event or problem first occurred, *and* to make a *statement of acceptance of self* in spite of the stated problem. The issue or aspect you've uncovered will form the first part of the Setup and so will vary with each client and each situation. The statement of acceptance can come in different forms as well.

Later we will learn how to use part of the Setup process to help clients reframe their issues, but the ultimate purpose of any reframe is to generate a broader understanding and, therefore, a greater acceptance of self and the world.

Carl Rogers, who is credited with pioneering the client-centered approach to therapy, is often quoted as saying, "The curious paradox is that when I accept myself just as I am, then I can change." His ideas are well reflected in EFT, since he promoted the idea of clients as the expert on thier own issues and the therapist as a guide (LaCombe, 2008). In level 1, you learned that the default acceptance of the Setup is "I deeply and completely accept myself." This default is a generic statement that applies to most situations. Any statement that creates an acceptance of self even though you have a problem can be used. Some clients will not be able to, or don't want to, say that they deeply and completely accept themselves. In addition, the repetitive nature of the default statement gets... well, repetitive. The important thing is to make some statement that resonates with the client.

There are infinite options for positive acceptance phrases that can accept self *in spite of* the problem. Many alternative statements are possible that could ring true to even the most reluctant or discerning client. Here are just a few examples:

- *I'm okay.*
- *That's okay.*
- *I'm okay with that.*
- *I can accept that I can't accept myself.*
- *I'll think about accepting myself later.*
- *I accept how I feel about it.*
- *I am still a really good person.*
- *I can accept parts of me but not that part.*
- *I count, too.*
- *I was doing the best I could at the time*

With a particularly reluctant client, you can address the nonacceptance, itself, as the specific problem to tap for. "Even though I don't accept myself, I accept that I don't accept myself." This may sound a bit odd, but it actually works *because it is the truth* – we believe *both of these* at the same time. We accept parts of us and not others. A few rounds of tapping on nonacceptance, using phrases such as "I don't accept myself, well, maybe a little bit, no, not at all, but I accept that I don't accept myself," should bring up something when you ask, "What comes up for you now? Is there any *part* of you that you can accept?"

Setups for Single Aspects

The goal of a Setup is both to acknowledge the problem and to accept the self in spite of having the problem. You can develop a Setup from any problem clients tell you. The simplest method is to create a new Setup for each aspect that comes up.

Simple Setups

Use a Setup such as "Even though I am angry with my sister for hitting me, I deeply and completely accept myself," and repeat it three times while tapping the chosen Setup point (Karate Chop point or Sore Spot). Then tap using the Reminder Phrase "angry at my sister." As you tap for the anger, a sense of rejection may become apparent. The Setup is then changed to follow the new emotional aspect of anger. The Setup then becomes "Even though I felt rejected by my sister, I deeply and completely accept myself anyway," repeated three times. Then tap on the Reminder Phrase "feel rejected."

The sense of rejection may then move to one of sadness for all you've missed by staying angry. The Setup becomes "Even though I missed so much and it makes me sad, I accept what happened and how I feel," repeated three times. Then tap on the Reminder Phrase "this sadness."

Let's say that tapping for the sadness does not relieve it. The sadness starts at an 8 and goes down to a 4. The second round of tapping would modify the Setup to "Even though I *still* have some of this remaining sadness, I deeply and completely accept myself anyway," repeated three times; then use the Reminder Phrase "this remaining sadness" as you tap.

There is often some resistance to giving up a problem. Using the phrases "still have some" and "this remaining" helps take care of the internal objections to resolving the problem completely. If this is still not effective, you can discover and tap specifically for additional factors and aspects supporting the resistance.

After tapping, when more information is needed for the next round, you can incorporate the question *"What comes up for you now?"* to bring out the next layer of the issue. As long as you keep finding aspects, continue the process, always with the goal of lowering the intensity around the issue while helping the client to get more and more specific.

Working this way is particularly useful when the client starts with a general Setup. Beginning with, for instance, "Even though I can't stick to my diet, I deeply and completely accept myself" in the first round will help lower the intensity around the topic of dieting, so that you can then use questions to get a more specific aspects of the problem. "What comes up for you now?" is a very effective start. Other similar questions that can be effective at this stage of the process are:
- *How do you know this is a problem?*
- *What happened to make you believe that?*
- *How do you feel about yourself when you ___?*
- *What is your family's view of ___?*
- *What is the downside of ___?*

Use the answers to the question to continue the process by modifying the Setup and repeat it three times while tapping the chosen Setup point. Then use a brief Reminder Phase based on the client's words and tap the points. Ask another question designed to get to something even more specific. "I can't stick to my diet" can become "Even though I feel guilty because I grabbed the last piece of cake, I deeply and completely accept myself." Modify the Reminder Phrase to "feel guilty" and repeat the Basic or Full Basic Recipe. Your goal each time is to calm the intensity around the issue and help the client to get to something more specific.

Extending the Setup Language

The simple default Setups for single aspects work very, very well. The *EFT Level 1 Comprehensive Training Resource* stressed the importance of working with one issue or aspect at a time as an effective way to ensure that all aspects have been cleared completely. Up to now, we have been tapping in a repetitive way for one aspect of one event and then moving on to the next aspect after the present aspect's intensity lowers. Sometimes, because a client is already tuned in to a specific event, extending the Setup language and Reminder Phrases to include different ways of viewing the same aspect or even including more than one aspect often resolves the entire event more quickly. This takes a bit of practice and a great deal of attention to the progress or delays of your client.

Extending the Setup language is an important skill, but one that many find daunting. One of the biggest fears for new learners of EFT is that they won't be able to find the "right" words. Books and articles that offer EFT scripts for tapping on specific issues are popular because people feel more confident with directions to follow. The downside of these scripts is that, in order to appeal to a broad audience, they must be generic and global. Following a script may *seem* fast and easy, but such scripts are usually not specific enough to address all the aspects around your or your client's particular issue. While you are learning, remember that you can always start with the client's words.

Ask the Client

Repeating the client's words for Setups and Reminder Phrases is an important and basic rule to success with EFT. Remember that EFT uses a client-centered approach and that creative wording is unnecessary for results. The client is the expert. You are the guide. All too often, as practitioners, we think we know best. We think we are the only one who can discover the underlying issues in our clients' problems. Asking your clients for their theories, however, is not only respectful, it also helps bring up more effective Setups.

- *What is your theory about what is causing this?*
- *What do you think this is all about?*
- *What do you imagine is causing this?*

Does your client have no idea? Try these options for working with issues when your client doesn't know:

- *Create an Answer.* Ask the client, "If you did know, what would it be?"
- *Just Guess.* Ask the client to take a wild guess as to what it could be.
- *Let's Pretend.* Ask the client to make up a story about it. Ask him to just pretend he knows and tell a story about it.
- *Tap for Not Knowing.* Ask the client to tap for "Even though I don't know why I have this problem...." This will normally allow something to come to the surface of consciousness.

The Right Words

The EFT Intermediate Library "Tutorial #4: Finding the Right Words," reinforces the idea that you develop "the right words" by listening carefully to your client. It advises that you must "understand the experience from their shoes. Ask as many questions as it takes to get to the specifics, and then you can use their words to help them recreate the event during the session. You will soon see that

each client has a different experience, and you may never need the same words twice." (Craig, 2008b, p. 3)

The tutorial goes on to caution against relying too much, too soon, on your own intuition. Though there are times when intuition is helpful in shifting your focus or direction, some people think that they only need to "produce the right words and the magic will happen." As a result, they may be inclined to listen too closely to their own intuition rather than listening to the client. EFT values the practitioner's intuitive instincts, but "Finding the Right Words" cautions that intuitive guidance needs a strong foundation of experience, communication skills, detective work, and social skills to be truly valuable (Craig, 2008b, p. 3).

Bringing in the Positive

One of the pitfalls to watch out for while looking for the right words is attempting to begin using positive statements too soon. Some inexperienced practitioners, and clients, resist what they see as "focusing on the negative" while tapping. Perhaps they are drawn to positive statements. Perhaps they are uncomfortable "dwelling on" the negative or they've heard about "positive thinking" and the "law of attraction." Or, perhaps, because we as practitioners all want the best for our clients, we may just want to help a client feel better and so be tempted to rush to bring in a positive statement long before it's appropriate.

As we begin to discuss extending Setups, you'll learn the *right* time to use positive statements: how to use them in regard to affirmations and how to use them to help clients reframe their perspective on an issue. Most of the positive statements practitioners make tend to be presented as reframes. We'll discuss this in more detail, but here we want to emphasize that timing is critical for all reframes. Introducing them too soon can cause resistance from the client and even a loss of rapport.

Until your client clears his negative belief, remember, and remind him if necessary, that we are not tapping to *reinforce* the negative; we are tapping for his *existing truth*. Acceptance of the reality of the issue is a prerequisite for changing it, so he must tap for his current reality before he taps for what he would like reality to be. The work of EFT is to clear the negative beliefs so that positive ones can begin to attract the things we want in life.

The client has to do this at his own pace. Resist the temptation to "talk" the client out of his negative belief, just because it's negative. Your task is to guide the client to find and tap for whatever aspects led to his current belief. If your client can't address a feeling or event and struggles to focus on the positive, it could be that he doesn't want to look at the real event or feeling when *that* may be precisely what needs to be looked at. Remember, your job is that of a guide dog, helping your clients safely down the path at their own pace. It may seem easier, sometimes, to jump straight to a positive statement rather than digging out the core issue, which may be buried under many layers, but until you find these core negative beliefs, the client's issues remain unresolved. Putting a positive spin on a client's issues before resolving them is just giving him a pep talk. He may feel good for a while after leaving your office, but the problem will soon confront him again, and he will be right back where he started.

Tapping on specific aspects that address core issues will lead the client to the natural cognitive shift that's needed. In other words, the positive will come naturally. You just need to *trust the process* and help your client to trust it, too.

Customizing the Setup

The EFT Intermediate Library "Tutorial #6: Customizing Your Setup Phrases" offers two ways to extend Setup language: the Extended Setup and the Setup/Reminder Combination. These two methods are used to address many or most of the aspects of a story or event, instead of picking one aspect of the story to focus on. Sometimes you will need to focus on one particular aspect at a time to release it fully, but often, when combining aspects in this way, events can be collapsed more quickly than addressing them one at a time.

Extended Setup

Customizing Setups for more than one aspect at a time begins, as always, with the client. The Extended Setup works by weaving wording from the client's story into Setup and Reminder Phrases. For the Extended Setup, the statement of the problem uses the overall problems as reported in the story; the Reminder Phrases use *several* key elements of the story instead of just one. To use this technique, as your client tells you a story, listen carefully. Note particularly any parts that bring up more intensity. You will develop the initial Setup by using many details of the story, but the Reminder Phrases will be taken from details that demonstrate the greater intensity.

Ann offers an illustration from her practice for the development of an Extended Setup: Jennie came to her session depressed because her mother was pushing her to attend an upcoming family reunion. Jennie didn't want to go because she was still very angry at her brother for the way he treated her as a child. "He was a jerk then, and he's a jerk now," she grumbled. Jennie began by relating an event when her brother hit her when she was nine and he was fourteen. When first asked to rank the intensity of her feeling (anger) around this event, she reported an 8.

Because the intensity was high, Ann began with a general Setup to lower intensity. She and Jennie tapped a couple of rounds on "this anger" until Jennie reported her intensity was down to a 6. As Jennie began to get more specific, bringing up more details in the story, Ann noted that some parts of the story brought up more intensity than others. Key wording for Setup and Reminder Phrases would come from these details.

Here are the details Jennie gave: "My mother went to run an errand and left me and my older brother and sister alone at home. I was sitting in the living room reading a book, minding my own business. My brother walked up and just backhanded me across the face *for no reason*." (Ann noted the greater emotion that came up when Jennie thought about this happening for no reason.) "I was so angry, but *I couldn't do anything*. He was much bigger and always won. He picked on me a lot. I just sat there thinking I'd like to kill him. I *couldn't tell my mother* because he'd just *hit me more* the next time she left."

The story Jennie told can be broken down into several aspects that can be woven into the initial Setup:

- *Mother left us alone.*
- *Minding my own business.*
- *He hit me for no reason.*
- *I was so angry.*
- *I couldn't do anything.*
- *He was much bigger.*
- *He always won.*
- *I wanted to kill him.*
- *I couldn't tell.*
- *He'd hit me more next time.*

Ann wove the story into the Setup, using key points to retell the major parts of the story, putting more emphasis on the parts that brought up the most emotion. Note that the acceptance part of the Setup can also change to reflect the client's truth.

"Even though my brother walked up and *hit me for no reason* when I was minding my own business after my mother left, and I was so angry because *I couldn't do anything* and he was bigger and always won, and even though *I couldn't even tell*

Mother because he'd just hit me again, I accept myself even though I sure don't accept him; he is such a jerk."

In Jennie's story, the statements "hit me for no reason," "I couldn't do anything," and "I couldn't tell my mother" created the most intensity for Jennie. For the Extended Setups, Ann, then, varied the Reminder Phrase to reflect those statements that caused the most intensity.

To compare use of the Extended Setup to simpler Setups, note that Jennie's presenting issue was that she was so angry with her brother that she didn't want to go to the reunion, and she tells the story of one event that supports her present anger. In the simple EFT Setup, you would pick one aspect of the time when her brother hit her for no reason. You would then ask Jennie what was the most difficult part of that event. When she said, "I couldn't do anything about it," your Reminder Phrase in the simple Setup would be "couldn't do anything." In contrast, in the Extended Setup, you will continue to use the presenting issue wording, "I am so angry at my brother," but you will also combine the details from the story. You will then use the "couldn't do anything" as well as the "he hit me for no reason" and "I couldn't tell mother" phrases for Reminder Phrases.

After the Extended Setup, using the Basic Recipe, Jennie and Ann tapped using variations on the most intense phrases as Reminders. Note that they tapped through all the points several times and that as Jennie provided feedback, Ann modified the wording.

Head point	So angry at my brother.
Eyebrow	Hit me for no reason.
Side of the eye	I was so angry.
Under the eye	I couldn't do anything.

Jennie nods and adds, "I was helpless to do anything about him."

Under the nose	I was helpless to do anything about him.
Chin	He hit me for no reason.
Collarbone	I was so angry.
Under arm	I was helpless to do anything.
Head point	I couldn't tell my mother.
Eyebrow	I couldn't hit him back.
Side of the eye	I couldn't do anything.
Under the eye	He was so much bigger.
Under the nose	He always won.
Chin	I was helpless to do anything
Collarbone	He hit me for *no* reason.

Jennie says, "It was so unfair."

Under arm	It was so unfair.
Head point	He hit me for *no* reason.

Jennie says, "He shouldn't have done that."

Eyebrow	He shouldn't have done that.
Side of the eye	It was so unfair.
Under the eye	I was helpless.
Under the nose	He hit me for no reason.
Chin	I was so angry.

Jennie says, "Why would he do that?"

Collarbone	Why would he do that?
Under arm	I couldn't tell my mother.
Head point	I felt so helpless.

Notice that the order of the phrases is not important. What's important is that all of Jennie's higher intensity statements were used and, whenever Jennie gave feedback phrasing, it was incorporated.

At this point, Ann asked Jennie to take a deep breath and then asked how she felt now when she thought of the event. Jennie said the anger at her brother was gone, "It is a 0." She went on to say, "My father always beat him. He was just taking out his anger on me." *Note that, as Jennie reached 0 intensity, she flowed naturally into her own cognitive shift.*

As Jennie breathed easier and talked about her brother differently, she still exhibited emotion around the idea that she'd been helpless, "He was really just a kid, too... but I was just nine, I couldn't do anything." Although Jennie's anger was relieved, Ann could see that Jennie's perception of her helplessness was still an issue. Jennie had trouble putting these feelings into words, so Ann asked her to "go inside" and identify where she felt the reaction in her body. Jennie said she felt the helplessness welling up in her throat as if an elephant were sitting on her chest. She gave the feeling an intensity level of 6. Jennie then tapped a couple of rounds using a simple Setup and Reminder Phrase, "this helplessness."

Jennie seemed to breathe easier for a moment, but then began to tear up again. Ann asked, "What's coming up for you now?"

Jennie's lip quivered, "Why would my mother leave me with him? She knew he was aggressive."

As children and, often, even as adults, we interpret everything as to how it relates to us. To get at these interpretations, Ann often asks the question, "What did that mean to you?"

With this question, Jennie began to cry, "I don't think my mother really cared what happened to me." As Jennie resolved the issue with her brother, another deeper core issue was revealed.

Setup/Reminder Combination

The Setup/Reminder Combination is similar to the Extended Setup except that *the extended phrase is carried through the tapping sequence,* so that there's no distinction between the Setup and the Reminder Phrases. As you develop the combination, there are no rules as to where to break the phrases or when to use them. Use your judgment and intuition as to what you feel works best for you and the client. Incorporate even more self-acceptance as you move through the process. As you tap, use either the Basic Recipe or the Full Basic Recipe with either of the customized Setup methods. Likewise, there's no rule about which point you start with. The Karate Chop point, Top of the Head, or, indeed, any point is fine. This example uses the Full Basic Recipe.

Head point	Even though my brother walked up and hit me for no reason,
Eyebrow	when I was minding my own business after my mother left,
Side of the eye	and I was so angry,
Under eye	because I couldn't do anything,
Under nose	because he was bigger and always won.
Collarbone	Even though I couldn't even tell Mother,
Under arm	because he'd just hit me again.
Thumb	*I accept myself, even though I sure don't accept him. He's such a jerk.*

Let's say Jennie nods vigorously at this point.
Use her feedback to begin the next phrase.

Index finger	Even though he is such a jerk and always has been,
Middle finger	And he probably always will be, *I accept myself anyway.*
Baby finger	He hit me for no reason, that's so unfair!

Jennie's mouth tightens as she nods again, so we reiterate that phrase.

Karate chop	Even though it was so unfair, my mother was gone and I couldn't do anything.
Head point	She left and he hit me and I couldn't do anything.
Eyebrow	*I accept myself anyway.*
Side of the eye	Even though he was a jerk and it was so unfair,
Under eye	*it's okay to feel like I feel.*
Under nose	Even though I was helpless to do anything about it,
Under chin	*I accept myself and how I feel, I am a good person.*
Collarbone	Even though it was so unfair. I was helpless to do anything about it.
Under arm	I was just nine years old, he was so much bigger and always won.

Thumb	I've carried that anger around for thirty years.
Index finger	*I am okay with how I feel 'cause that is how I feel.*
Middle finger	And it was a long time ago,
Baby finger	And I survived,
Karate chop	Even though that doesn't make it right. Other big brothers are jerks, too, just like mine.

Throughout the process, you listen to and watch your client carefully so you know how well your words are being accepted by the client. Modify what you say according to the client's verbal and nonverbal feedback. *Keep tapping on the points until the story and the client's reactions reach a logical conclusion.* You do not need to end on any specific EFT point. Repeat tapping as you summarize the story on the points as often as you feel necessary to lower intensity. Add in more points or the Full Basic Recipe, if you wish, or if progress is slow. Continue going through the points until the client exhibits little or no emotion in response to them. Stop and test for any intensity on any part of the story. Because you are using more words and covering more aspects, you will tap through the points several times before stopping to check the intensity level. When the client appears calm, stop and test where she is on each of the aspects of the story.

Write down your clients' specific wording so you can use those exact words for testing. You can ask, "How's the helpless feeling?" or "Is the unfair feeling still as strong?" to check the progress and to identify where you should focus. Encourage your client to add to the story or to share other feelings and insights as they come up. In Jennie's case, what came up was the beginning of understanding toward her brother ("Our father was gone so much and when he came home, it was always my brother he picked on") and a sense of being abandoned by her mother ("She knew he was aggressive towards me; why did she leave us alone? I just don't think my mother cared about me or what I needed.")

Always remember to get an intensity level. Remember you can use the VOC scale, rather than the SUD scale, any time it seems more appropriate. You might ask, "How true is the statement that your mother didn't care about what you needed?" For the next tapping round, no matter what type of Setup you use, you would include the new information emphasizing the feelings of abandonment and not being cared for by her mother. After tapping, test again.

If a client reports a 0, begin to test each part of the story, each part of the event, each emotion. Even though you have been tapping for the entire event at the same time, you want to test each part to ensure there is no remaining intensity anywhere. Ask about sights, sounds, feelings, smells, and tastes, and tap on any remaining unresolved aspects. Because *the language used in extending the Setup is not focusing on one specific aspect, testing to ensure all parts of the issue are resolved becomes even more important.* After using either of the two extended language Setups, make sure you review each element in the story with the client to ensure it is all clear. Make sure the issue is completely resolved; *there is no substitute for testing for each aspect.*

If the entire story is not down to 0, continue to tap through the points as often as needed, using either the Extended Setup or the Setup/Reminder Combination. When you feel the client has made obvious progress, check the intensity level, either after each set of tapping rounds or after several rounds. Pay close attention to your client, noting where the strongest emotion comes up and focusing on that part of the event to create another Setup. Use this part as a more frequent Reminder Phrase to clear any remaining intensity around that aspect. You can use the Watch the Movie Technique or the Tell the Story technique to ensure there are no lingering aspects.

If something "pops up," check for new aspects, always asking "What comes up for you now?" when you see evidence of new emotion. Many times, a hidden aspect will pop up when all apparent aspects have been resolved. Use the client's answer to create another Setup, whether you use the one aspect Setup or an extended Setup or combination Setup/Reminder Phrase.

If you are in the middle of dealing with one aspect when another event pops into the client's mind, make a note to come back to it after you're sure that the event and aspects you are already working on are all down to a 0. If intensity levels are not dropping, then it's possible that you need to resolve the event that "popped up" before the present one can resolve. The *general* rule is to clear the first event and all its aspects before moving on. Like any rule, however, it is meant to be broken. There are times when the new aspect becomes more important than the initially presented event or aspect. Use your intuition, *or ask the client,* which event or aspect should be addressed now. If you do need to jump to a different aspect or event, always return to the unresolved aspect or event after clearing the new one.

Because it is possible to collapse some issues quickly using extended language and the Basic Recipe, it could seem easy. Inexperienced EFTers may assume this is *the way* to do EFT. They may spend their time working to get more details into every Setup. Keep in mind that, sometimes, *you can try to do too much in one round of tapping*, so always test the results and be ready to go back to dealing with one specific aspect at a time.

 ## Test Your Knowledge

1. True or false? The specific language used for the acceptance part of the Setup is less important than assuring that whatever is said is a statement of acceptance that feels comfortable for the client.

2. Which of the following is not an important step to address before starting a tapping sequence?
a. Identify a specific problem or mind-body connection.
b. Recap the last EFT session.
c. Create a targeted Setup.
d. Get an intensity level.
e. None of the above.

3. True or false? After tapping, if a client reports a 0 in intensity, it is okay to take her word for it.

4. True or false? When using the Setup and Reminder Phrase combination, you can modify your words based on the verbal and nonverbal cues of the client.

5. True or false? The only difference in the Extended Setup and the Setup/Reminder Combination is that one uses the Basic Recipe and the other uses the Full Basic Recipe.

Answers can be found in Appendix E

Chapter 8 – Composing New Writing

Framing, in construction, sets up the boundaries, limits, or goals of a project. Ultimately, the framing determines the outcome. If you begin a building by framing a house, when it's finished, it'll be a house; it won't be a railroad station. Extending our palace metaphor, if we frame a closet, we won't end up with a palace. In the same way, *our core beliefs frame and limit our experience*. If we set out believing we'll live paycheck to paycheck all our lives, it's likely that is what we'll end up doing.

As we've seen, it's the writing on our walls, our core beliefs, that serve to frame our view of the world, limiting our potential for a productive, happy life. The role of EFT is to uncover and, if necessary, erase or change these core beliefs by dealing with the specific events that lie at their origins. When our emotional reactions to these events are neutralized, what happens *naturally* is a cognitive shift: a change in our perspectives on ourselves, the situation, the people involved, and the world. Recall Craig's words, that the "cognition change is the true bottom line" (nda, p. 138). This cognitive shift is the ultimate goal of EFT.

Reframes

Although, the cognitive shift is a natural result of the EFT process, there are tools for facilitating easier or faster shifts. One way of doing this is to change clients' framing of an event to change their perspective on it. To illustrate how a change in framing can affect your perspective, imagine being given a time frame for finishing a task at work. If you have an hour to finish, you will feel and act differently than if you have a month. Changing the time frame will change the choices you make. The same thing happens in life even when we aren't aware of the way our beliefs are framing our choices (Ellerton, 2004).

In EFT, a *reframe* is any statement that presents a new way of looking at an issue. *Reframing* is offering a new way of thinking in an effort to encourage a change in the client's perception. A change in the perspective on a specific event can lead to a cognitive shift that changes or erases the core belief that has been supporting the client's presenting problem. Having a client see his or her situation from a broader perspective is the goal of any type of therapy. The cognitive shift is the goal, but only the client can make that shift. The right reframe offered at the right time encourages the shift and speeds the process.

Reframing is not unique to EFT. Craig learned the technique, initially, from his background in Neuro-Linguistic Programming, and the idea is common to other therapies as well. What is new with EFT is the practice of reframing *while* tapping. As Craig (2009) described it in "The Timeless EFT Principles," the tapping "radically improves how well reframes 'land' with the client." The mechanism for this improvement isn't well understood, so there may be other factors at work. It appears however, that as tapping decreases the emotional intensity around an event, the client, at minimum, becomes more open to receiving a new perspective on the event. For this reason, we usually don't attempt a reframe until the client reports an intensity that is quite low, perhaps 3 or less.

Those of you who have seen experienced practitioners intuitively offer skillful reframes may be concerned that you won't be able to come up with the right words. Don't despair. Remember it's the client who makes the shift and it's a natural process. Just go after all the related aspects and events and your clients will get there on their own, but remember, too, that reframing is an advanced technique. Craig writes in the EFT Intermediate Library "Tutorial #7: Reframes" that you are ready to learn reframes "as soon as you have solid experience with the basic EFT procedure, can consistently collapse Tabletops, and can erase the writing on your clients' walls with standard EFT alone."

To understand and use reframes, you must first be adept at developing Setups and Reminder Phrases, and at modifying those phrases as the process progresses. The reframe is added to the Setup. Craig writes in "The Timeless EFT Principles" of his discovery of this technique: "Once I learned to customize the Default Setup Phrase...and collapse emotional intensity more completely, I began adding Reframes to see if I could shift the client's perspective in a healthier direction. The results were astounding, and the degree of cognitive shift that I was able to produce was yet another important innovation to the EFT process."

The reframe generally replaces the acceptance portion of the Setup. For example, when a client has tapped and has low intensity around "Even though my brother gave me a black eye when I was eight, I deeply and completely accept myself," the client may be ready to reframe the event to "Even though my brother hit me, he was an unhappy angry kid…"

Remember, it's the client who makes the shift. The most effective reframes are those that come from the client. If you find yourself struggling to come up with reframes, relax and remember that questions are *so* powerful. Questions allow clients to create their own answers as they have to question and describe their own perceptions. Many practitioners get bogged down trying to create a brilliant reframe for the client when their time and energy could be better spent asking questions as simple as "What comes up for you now?" after tapping on an issue, then going where the client leads next.

Clients often create their own natural reframes since it's a natural process to make that cognitive shift. As the emotion starts to recede, the client may offer her own reinterpretation of the event: "Even though my brother gave me a black eye when I was eight, well…he was only ten…my kids fought with each other when they were that age…" One of the easiest ways you can come up with the best reframes is to recognize and help your clients recognize their *own* cognitive shifts by pointing out the changes in their descriptions and interpretations of their own stories.

The "Right" Reframe

Reframing is a powerful tool. Developing effective reframes can help move a client on toward a successful resolution. The client wants resolution and reframing is part of the natural process. So can you do it "wrong"? Absolutely. Doing it "wrong" is letting the writing on your walls get in the way, pushing your own values and beliefs on the client, rather than meeting the client "where he is" and guiding the client to a healthier perspective for *him*. You wouldn't state a reframe, for instance, to a non-Christian client as, "Even though my brother gave me a black eye when I was eight, Jesus tells us to turn the other cheek…"

To ensure that you don't do it "wrong," let's borrow a procedure from the medical profession. As a part of quality assurance for patients, nurses are taught to check five "rights" before administering any medication:
- *Right patient*
- *Right route*
- *Right dose*
- *Right time*
- *Right medication*

We can adapt these five "rights" to our discussion of using reframes with your clients.

Successfully suggesting a reframe that will be accepted by your client means using the right reframe for that specific client, when they are ready to hear and accept it, with just the right amount of modified/new concepts introduced and using the correct method (i.e., acceptable words, humor, strong emphasis, quiet tone, etc.) to state it. When you get it all "right," the client accepts the reframe and moves on quickly either to total resolution or to the next event or issue.

What happens if the reframe you use is not the right reframe at the right time for that client? Usually *nothing* happens. The reframe won't "land" with the client. Often, when there is strong rapport, a client will tell you that what you said wasn't right. If you have developed both strong rapport and a safe environment for the client to disagree or correct you, the client will simply say, "I don't feel that way" or "That doesn't fit." If this happens, you can consider it a good sign that you have developed a strong positive relationship with the client. Good work! React positively, then simply let it go and move on.

If you have strong rapport with your client, you will be able to offer a reframe that doesn't "land," with no harm done, although the client may temporarily lose focus while trying to connect with what you said. This "confusion" may last only a few seconds as the client corrects you and you back up and try again. This is why it's so important to make sure that your client feels comfortable enough within the relationship to correct you. If the client feels pushed, or *if your reframe indicates to your client that you were not really listening, that you don't respect him, or are trying to move him to a particular resolution too quickly, you can lose the client and possibly do some harm to him in the process.* Remember that your clients always need to be empowered to feel that they can solve their own issues. Be sure that you aren't projecting the writing on *your* walls onto your clients. You don't want any client, even one that leaves, to go away doubting his own perceptions because of a hasty attempt at reframe or a reframe offered to meet *your* needs and not the client's.

Remember, this is an important reason to *do your own work*. There are many ways that a practitioner can project her own beliefs onto a reframe. A practitioner could assume that everyone has similar family experiences. For example, a client presents saying that she's afraid of men. The practitioner, knowing nothing about the client's history, attempts a reframe: "Even though I'm afraid of men, my father is a good man..." The practitioner might imply disrespect, making the client feel inferior or "crazy." Or the problem may be "I'm afraid to fly" and the practitioner tries the reframe "Even though I'm afraid to fly, I remember that it's all in my head." These examples are not reframes; they are instances of the practitioner pushing her own agenda.

In the DVD *Pursuit of Excellence* (Adams, 2009a), Ann gives an example of a practitioner who "lost" a client by pushing his own agenda in giving a reframe that didn't land. Years ago, Ann was supervising a new practitioner in a training session when the client said, "It [the emotional pain] hurts so bad, I just want to shut down and stop feeling anything." This statement must have triggered the writing on the walls of the practitioner because he proposed the Setup "Even though I hurt so badly I want to stop feeling, and I know I won't do that because feelings are important, I deeply and completely accept myself." This is not a reframe; this is imposing values on the client. The practitioner didn't notice, as we often don't when we are in our own world. Ann stopped them and gently suggested that if the client had the ability to stop feeling, she would have done so in the twenty years she'd had her problem. Wishing that you could stop feeling lousy is certainly a rational response if there seems to be no other solution. *Who in her right mind wants to feel bad?* The Setup was changed to "Even though I hurt so badly I want to stop feeling, I deeply and completely accept myself anyway."

The moral of this story shows up in the comments the client made to Ann later. She thanked Ann for stopping the session. Her comment was, "That was right on! I wasn't being heard and felt like he was taking me where I didn't want to go." Note that she made this comment to Ann, not the practitioner. *Leading breaks rapport. Leading shuts down real communication. Leading can lose your client and, because leading means you were following your own agenda rather than listening to the client, you won't even realize why you lost him.*

Remember that problems can be resolved using EFT even if reframes are never introduced. The client will come to them naturally on his own.

Using Humor and Exaggeration

Gary Craig used a variety of reframes in his demonstrations to help clients see the writing on their walls for the illogical beliefs they often are. Craig's strategy was to take a negative belief and create a Setup from it: "Even though I believe ___, I deeply and completely accept myself." He would often go on to rationalize the belief: "I created this belief for a good reason and it has served me well. But now maybe it is not working quite as well as it has been." In the EFT Intermediate Library "Tutorial #7: Reframes" and in his DVDs, Craig developed one of his hallmark techniques, exaggerating a negative belief until the client could not help but see the humor in it.

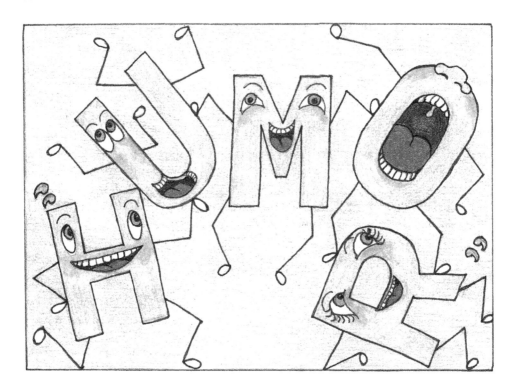

He used several strategies, including eroding the authority of the belief and reducing it to the ridiculous, to help his clients naturally shift the belief to a healthier one. For instance, with a client who had a traumatic relationship with his mother that ended in his belief that all women were scary, Craig might say, "Even though I learned by first grade that relationships don't work, it's vitally important that I keep believing the relationship advice of a six-year-old because everyone knows that six-year-olds are experts on adult relationships."

After slipping in a Setup like this one, Craig might ask, "Is this logical?" The client would almost always answer with a resounding "No!" Our conscious minds recognize when our beliefs are not actually true, but until the unconscious mind erases it and our bodies no longer feel it, the irrational belief (and, often, irrational behavior) remains. If you attempt strong reframing techniques such as these, remember to offer the reframes toward the end of sessions when emotional intensity has dissipated (Craig recommends a 3 or below) and the client is more likely to be ready for a cognitive shift.

Karin was demonstrating using EFT for a snake phobia. The woman said she had never been able to look at a photo she had of her son with a snake around his neck, taken at a petting zoo. As Karin continued using EFT, she tried the reframe "All snakes in the entire world bite and strangle" because the picture the woman had of her son obviously seemed to indicate otherwise. To Karin's surprise, the woman nodded her head in full agreement, "Yes, *all* snakes in the *entire* world bite and strangle." Karin had attempted the reframe too soon. She was able to continue tapping without losing rapport, however. Later in the session, Karin tried the exact same wording and added, "Is that still true?" The woman slowed her tapping to think and said, "Well...maybe not that *one* snake in that picture with my son." So they continued, "Even though I thought *all* snakes in the world bite and strangle, I now know there is at least *one* snake that doesn't bite and strangle." This became the turning point in the session, after which the client's phobia lessened quickly.

Reframing with Qualifiers

Careful reframes with qualifiers is another way to combine listening to the client with the "right words." If the client says, "It's never worked before," adding "so far" can begin to shift the client's thinking toward a reframe that will serve her better. Possible qualifiers are might, probably, may, think about, could, will, possibly, yet, possibility of, maybe, someday, and consider.

CHAPTER 8 – COMPOSING NEW WRITING

 # Test Your Knowledge

1. True or false? In EFT, a reframe is any statement that presents a new way of looking at an issue and, when used skillfully, can encourage a cognitive shift.

2. True or false? When our emotional reactions to events are neutralized, what happens *naturally* is a cognitive shift.

3. Which of the following is _not_ true?
a. A reframe generally replaces the acceptance portion of the Setup.
b. Reframes are generally introduced when the intensity is 3 or below.
c. Changing the client's "framing" of an event can change his perspective of it.
d. Rapport is not a factor in reframes.

True or False? Craig recommends you have solid EFT experience using standard EFT alone to collapse events and issues before beginning to use reframes.

Answers can be found in Appendix E

Chapter 9 – Blocked Doorways

Single traumatic events are effectively neutralized with EFT. But researchers (Wells, Polglase, Andrews, Carrington, & Baker, 2003; Swingle, Pulos, & Swingle, 2005; Rowe, 2005; Church, Geronilla, & Dinter, 2009; Karatzias, et al., 2011) have begun to explore the efficacy of EFT for treating chronic issues, as well, and many clients seek help for the things in their lives that they feel have blocked them from fully realizing their potential. It is essential for the aspiring practitioner to learn techniques that specifically address certain common types of issues. The following sections show you how to apply the principles and techniques we've discussed to specific types of issues. Here you will also see Ann and Karin handle different levels of intensity in their clients. The case studies presented are not straight factual accounts of any one case but, rather, a compilation of experiences (all names and identifying details have been changed) told in narrative form to illustrate the techniques used.

PTSD

As evident from its name, posttraumatic stress disorder (PTSD) happens after a traumatic event. The event could have been a real threat or an event the sufferer perceived as a threat. PTSD symptoms can show up very soon after the event or take years to develop. The DSM-IV-TR states that, with PTSD, the individual "has experienced, witnessed, or been confronted with an event or events that involve actual or threatened death or serious injury, or a threat to the physical integrity of oneself or others. The person's response involved intense fear, helplessness, or horror" (U.S. Department of Veteran Affairs). Recall, however, that the effect on a person is a result of the *interpretation* of the event, the result of the writing on the walls *about* the event, not the event itself. While most people would agree that armed combat is objectively traumatic, any event can be perceived as traumatic and can result in PTSD or other negative effects. The event does not even have to occur to the person affected. People can feel threatened even if they only observe an event, or just hear about a death, serious harm, or threat that happened to someone else.

The effects of PTSD can be devastating. PTSD sufferers may reexperience the event over and over through obsessive thoughts, nightmares, or repetitive flashbacks. They may have trouble sleeping. They may become hypervigilant to similar triggers (sounds or scenes that in some way trigger the memory). They may avoid any situation that could trigger their anxiety or other reaction. They could have a startle response even when the danger is not present. They can become detached or estranged from other people. They may experience a reduced ability to feel emotions (especially those associated with intimacy).

When they survived the event and others didn't, there can be significant guilt about surviving or about things they had to do in order to survive. They may develop a social phobia, agoraphobia, or other phobias related to triggers of the trauma. They may suffer from panic attacks, depression, substance abuse, and obsessive-compulsive behaviors.

PTSD Case Study – Raina

PTSD can have many layers (aspects) that need to be addressed, each in turn, to relieve the symptoms. For example, Raina came to see Ann Adams because she was having nightmares and having trouble taking care of her children. Raina's fiancé had been killed in an automobile accident while traveling home from a fishing trip six months earlier. Raina was camping with her children when the police came to tell her the news. She told Ann that, as they told her what happened, she pictured the accident and, in the next months, she replayed her version of what must have occurred over and over in her head. She began to startle every time she heard an ambulance, saw an ambulance, or thought about an ambulance. Anytime she heard an accident reported on the news, passed a hospital, or saw a wrecked vehicle, she would relive the picture she'd created in her head of Charlie being taken out of the wreck and carried to the hospital in an ambulance.

Her reaction had many layers. She was frightened of car accidents and ambulances, but she also felt very guilty that she had not tried to talk Charlie out of going. She felt that she should have been with him. "I should have stopped him or I should have gone with him." Her grief and depression was affecting her ability to care for her children and she was worried that she couldn't pull herself out of it. She said she was mostly unresponsive to her children and, recently, when her mother had come to the house and ended up yelling at her to "get a grip," she hadn't even been able to respond to that. "I just sat there numb," she said.

Raina met the criteria for PTSD as stated in the DSM-IV-TR. To Raina, the event engendered fear, helplessness, and horror. She had no strategy for dealing with the unexpected news of Charlie's death.

When Raina first came to see Ann, she was already obviously upset. Ann first showed her how the constricted breathing exercise could help calm her. As Raina began to tell her story, an ambulance raced by outside, sirens blaring. Raina jumped and started to cry. Since Raina was already distressed, testing for her intensity level was skipped; Ann assumed an intensity of 10 for Raina. They started tapping together.

Ann asked Raina to tap for "Even though I jump every time an ambulance goes by, I deeply and completely accept myself and my jumpiness." They tapped all the points, including the 9 Gamut, then tapped all the points again, while using Reminder Phrases like "This jumpiness, the sirens make me jump, I think about Charlie, I picture him in the ambulance, I can't get it out of my head, it goes over and over."

When they stopped, Ann asked Raina to assess her progress, "If you were a 10 when we started, what intensity would you be now?" Raina said with a bit of surprise, "I feel much less jumpy inside; I'd say I was a 3."

Ann then used questions to check for aspects. She asked, "As you think about the siren now, what comes up for you?" Raina started to cry again and said that when she thought of the ambulance, she thought about Charlie being all alone. "What does that mean to you?" Ann asked. Raina answered, "I couldn't be with him. He died all alone. I should have been there."

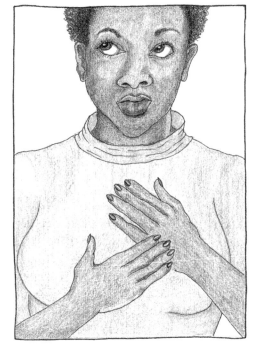

Many Reminder Phrases came up for this aspect: "He was all alone. I wasn't there. He died alone; I can't stand it. I wanted to be there. I couldn't be there. He was hurt. I wasn't there, I feel so guilty. I should have gone. I should have stopped him." Ann and Raina tapped all the points, several times, ending with the 9 Gamut Procedure and then the points one more time.

Ann watched Raina for physical manifestations of changes in how she was feeling. Raina relaxed more in her chair and her face became calmer. She stopped crying. Here breathing became fuller and deeper. When asked, she now reported the intensity was at a 3 when she thought about Charlie being alone.

They then tapped separate rounds for various aspects of the delivery of the news by the police, which led Raina to remember the reactions of her children, then to seeing Charlie's body, then to the funeral. Toward the end of the first session, another ambulance siren sounded. Raina grimaced but didn't startle. Ann went back to check on the aspects covered during the session. Raina reported 0 or low numbers. They made a list of what had not been completed to 0.

Ann asked what the biggest learning was that Raina was taking from the session and what she'd like to focus on the next session. "That tapping can make me calmer," she said. "And I'd like to work on feeling so guilty. I know logically I am not responsible but I feel like I am." Raina felt less triggered by the idea that Charlie was alone but still felt higher intensity around the idea that she should have prevented it somehow. Ann gave Raina an "EFT on a Page" handout and they talked about times Raina could tap during the week whenever she felt any jumpiness or anxiety.

The second session started with Raina's report of her week. She said she was still more aware of sirens than she had been before the accident, but she didn't jump or feel like crying every time she heard one. She said she had been able to pay more attention when her children talked to her, but she was still depressed much of the time. She had tapped a few times during the week and felt it had calmed her.

Ann reminded Raina that she'd said she wanted to work on her feeling that she was somehow responsible for the accident and asked if that was still her priority. When Raina, nodded, Ann continued, "You told me last week that you realize, rationally, you weren't responsible, but yet you still believe you are. Tell me more about that."

Raina said if she'd gone on the trip, they would have driven their other car, which was newer and safer. (The accident happened because a wheel came off Charlie's old truck.) Ann asked, "What made you decide not to go?"

"Charlie said I could come with him, but it was a bunch of guys that have been fishing together for years. I thought they'd be happier if it was just a guy thing. And I would have had to leave my kids. My parents wanted to go visit friends that weekend. So we all agreed. It seemed better for everyone. I'd take the kids camping and Charlie would meet us in the park after the fishing trip."

"So you all talked about the trip and decided together what would be best?"

"Yes," Raina agreed.

Ann noticed that Raina was really talking about two different aspects. She pointed out to Raina that she had a choice. "Looks like we have two parts to this. We could tap for your belief that you could have prevented the accident, or we can explore you feeling like *you* are at fault for making the decision that you are saying you *both* made *together*. Which would you like to work on now?" When clients bring up more than one topic, help them clarify any discrepancies in what they are telling you. You might say, "I'm confused about [this] because, before, you said [that]." Ask them to clear up the "confusion." Ask which statement is the "right" one or which statement they want to address.

Raina said she wanted to work on feeling she could have prevented the accident. Ann asked Raina how true the statement was that she could have prevented the accident. "About 95 percent," Raina said. They tapped a few more rounds using phrases like "I could have stopped him if I'd been there, I could have prevented the accident, Charlie would still be here, I wasn't there, I should have been there, I feel so guilty, I am responsible, if I'd been there it wouldn't have happened, I just wanted him to be happy, I thought all the guys would have a better time without me around, I should have gone. I could have prevented the accident." After a couple of rounds, Raina stopped.

She'd said that it was a guy thing, that her parents had a life, too, and that her kids were better off camping with her. She now told how she and Charlie had talked about the plans and had agreed on what they would do. "How responsible do you feel now for the accident?" Ann asked.

"I couldn't have stopped it. Charlie wanted to go. I guess I only believe I could have prevented it maybe now 30 percent. What came up was that I remembered Charlie talking about taking the car in to the shop the week before. He didn't tell me he took it, though, so I guess he didn't." Raina stopped with a new thought, "Oh no, why didn't I make sure he took it to the shop?"

Ann asked how she could have "made" him. Raina seemed stumped a minute, "I could've reminded him."

"Was Charlie ordinarily a responsible person?" Ann asked.

Raina responded, "Oh yes, he was really good about taking care of things. I guess he was just busy and thought it could wait. I should have reminded him."

Ann said, "What does it mean to you that you didn't remind him?"

Raina's eyes filled with tears, "I could have prevented the accident if I'd made him take the truck in. If I'd have bugged him, he would have done it."

They tapped for, "Even though I should have reminded him, I deeply and completely accept myself and that I didn't. Even though I am responsible because I didn't remind him, I accept myself anyway. Even though I feel I could have done something to prevent this, I accept my limitations as a human being, I have a job and two kids and a dog and volunteer work for the club. I was doing the best I could; Charlie was doing the best he could."

Ann used a combination Setup and Reminder Phrase, using part of the Setup wording *as* the Reminder Phrase, then during the last round of tapping, when Raina was obviously calmer, Ann added another reframe, "Even though I should have reminded him, he always did *everything* I asked right away *when* I asked, *all* the time, and *never* put anything off, or forgot to do what I asked."

Raina laughed, "I wish." The reframe helped Raina realize that reminding Charlie to take the truck in might not have been as effective as she'd been telling herself it would've been.

When they stopped to check in, Raina made her own cognitive shift. She said she had been doing the best she could and thought Charlie was, too. "We both worked so hard. We were so looking forward to this week off with us both doing our own thing and then getting back together."

She said she still had about 10 percent on feeling responsible because she didn't prevent the accident.

Ann asked, "What is it that keeps you at 10 percent?"

Raina responded, "I just think I could have done *something* to keep it from happening."

As you can see, there are many layers to the onion with PTSD. Patience, gentle questioning, persistence, and dedication to working with all aspects and related events are important.

Test Your Knowledge

1. All of the following are true of PTSD except
a. PTSD is caused by personally experiencing a life-threatening event.
b. PTSD symptoms show up after trauma.
c. PTSD is often associated with guilt.
d. PTSD can cause sufferers to be hypervigilant.

2. True or false? A person with PTSD can suffer from panic attacks, depression, substance abuse, and obsessive-compulsive behaviors.

Answers can be found in Appendix E

Phobias

"Phobia" is from the Greek word for fear. Phobias tend to be long lasting, rarely resolve on their own, can be intense, and are always irrational. In other words, phobias are characterized by the irrational fear of something that is not actually dangerous or happening to you at the time of the fear. If you have a fear response to something dangerous, it's a fear, not a phobia. Phobias come in many forms. Indeed, people can develop a phobia of just about anything. You can be afraid of any object (e.g., consecotaleophobia – fear of chopsticks), any place (e.g., ecclesiophobia – fear of churches), any animal (e.g., agrizoophobia – fear of wild animals), a state of being (e.g., isolophobia – fear of being alone), people (e.g., pedophobia – fear of children), something that might happen (e.g., molysmophobia – fear of contamination), colors (e.g., xanthophobia – fear of yellow), or numbers (numerophobia).

Whatever the presented phobia, whether it's a common one, like public speaking, spiders, or snakes, or one most people have never heard of, the process for dealing with it using EFT is always the same. Have the person think about the object of their fear. Rate the intensity at the thought of beginning to work on this issue and then start tapping. People with long-term phobias have often developed many coping skills for dealing with their fears. If a person has her life activities organized around avoiding a phobia, for instance, she may actually resist the idea of taking away the phobia. Go slowly and begin by addressing very minor parts of the problem. Gentle Techniques are very useful here.

As you work, clarify as many aspects and potential triggers for the phobia as you can. Ask questions. People shy away from thinking in too much detail about the object of their phobia, so they rarely think about how it makes their bodies feel or what *exactly* it is about the object that frightens them. Try to find the aspects that most trigger the client's reaction. Is it the fact that the spider is big? Is it that it has many legs? That the legs are hairy? Each detail can be an aspect to tap on. In most cases of phobia, we only have the client imagine the trigger as we tap with them. Only when the client feels ready, do we bring in a picture or a toy to represent the phobia (e.g., a big hairy plastic spider). These should be brought into the session as a test and only after the intensity on all aspects seems to have been cleared. Often the image or the representation will uncover more aspects to tap for. Treat all the aspects you can find before attempting to address the trigger in vivo.

Phobia Case Study – Sunnie

Sunnie came to see Karin because she was afraid to leave her home. She was able to force herself to leave to go to familiar areas close by, like the grocery store, a local restaurant, church, and the homes of nearby relatives and friends.

Driving was very difficult for her and she had to rely on others. Sunnie was tired of what she called "this artificial limitation" on her life. She couldn't rationalize her feelings and she was deeply afraid they would get worse. She had been to a therapist, but it hadn't helped much. Talking to her therapist had made her feel a little better for a short time after each session, but the fear was always with her. A friend told her about Karin and how she used a very different method for resolving problems.

Sunnie had her husband drive her to the first appointment. Although EFT can be done over the phone, Sunnie was determined to overcome her fear and forced herself to go to Karin's office. After introductions, Karin gave a brief overview of EFT, building a bridge by saying EFT was like acupuncture for the emotions but without the needles and sharing that EFT is still considered an experimental technique. Karin helped Sunnie experience the results of tapping by working with an emotional reaction Sunnie had to a movie she'd seen recently on TV.

Note: Using EFT on something small and not very important to Sunnie helped make her more comfortable with the newness of EFT, with tapping, both in general and with Karin.

When Karin felt that Sunnie was ready, she began to ask questions. As she did, she was careful that Sunnie never felt she was being interrogated. Karin worked to build rapport with her new client by emphasizing that she was asking Sunnie questions so she could "walk in your shoes," so she could understand Sunnie's own thoughts surrounding the problem, and so she could understand the feeling of fear and the impact it had on Sunnie's life.

Karin asked questions like "Because I don't feel what you feel when I leave my house, what words can you use to describe your feelings when you think about leaving your house? What are you afraid will happen if you leave? If that thing happens, what's the impact on you and your family? How do you get through those feelings when you do leave – what do think or say to yourself? What's the feeling in your body when you get back into your home?" Sunnie was surprised when she found she'd never thought about these questions and that she had to think as she tried to answer. But as Karin listened, Sunnie said she felt heard and understood, and since she'd never considered these questions before, she actually found this very enlightening.

Sunnie was fairly calm during the questioning, even, at times, seeming to enjoy the chance to think about her issue this way. A few times, she began to get upset or frightened. Karin always stopped and tapped with Sunnie until the intensity lessened. Initially, no particular event surfaced. Karin continued to ask questions following logical paths, exhibiting her genuine concern and curiosity. One path led to the core issue.

Karin: What bad thing could happen if you leave the house?

Sunnie: I could die.

Karin: Are you afraid of dying?

Sunnie: Not really.

Karin: What bad thing would happen if you die?

Sunnie: Well, my family would be left alone.

Karin: (Karin could see that the thought didn't really upset Sunnie.)
             How does that make you feel?

Sunnie: Well, it's sad, but they'd be fine. I've prepared for that already.

Karin: What other bad or scary thing would happen if you die?

Sunnie: Well, I'd meet the Lord.

Karin: And why is that bad or scary?

Suddenly Sunnie began to sob big heavy sobs and was barely able to breathe. Although Sunnie was clearly distressed and their rapport was strong, Karin still followed the preferred practice of asking Sunnie's permission to touch her. Karin did not break rapport, and she elicited an answer before continuing.

She touched Sunnie's hand. "Sunnie, can I tap on you?" Sunnie let out a yes while sobbing. Karin started tapping with no words. Alternatively, Karin could've asked permission when she was introducing EFT at the beginning of the session, but even when you have prior permission, it is still a good idea to ask before touching a client who is visibly upset.

Karin started to use words, "I'll meet the Lord," while tapping on each point. Sunnie kept crying, but Karin observed her breathing easier. Karin asked, "What will happen when you meet the Lord, Sunnie?"

Sunnie began to cry harder and said, "I'll find out." They tapped while Karin repeated, "I'll find out." Sunnie took a deep breath. "What will you find out, Sunnie?" Karin asked gently, while she continued tapping on Sunnie, but added, "You don't need to tell me if you don't want to."

But Sunnie answered, "That I forgot something. You see, how can I know? I try to follow Jesus in everything I do. But what if I get to heaven and there's something I missed?" Sunnie started crying again.

Karin continued quietly to tap on Sunnie until Sunnie stopped crying. As Sunnie gained control, she was able to take over tapping on herself. Karin went back to tapping on her own points, mirroring Sunnie. Karin feels it is important to empower clients as much as possible. She wants them to know that they are in control of their own healing. She wants clients to feel comfortable when they leave her office, knowing that they can go home and use EFT on their own. Some practitioners find, however, that always tapping *on* their clients works best for them. For example, EFT Master Emma Roberts works with many clients who have cancer. She feels that the touch and connection provided by tapping on her clients is very important to their progress.

As Sunnie seemed ready, Karin continued, "When is the first time you remember feeling you might miss something that could keep you out of heaven?"

Sunnie looked a bit confused for a moment and then suddenly remembered a time she'd been a little girl playing in the backyard. A neighborhood child wanted to play with Sunnie's new doll and Sunnie wouldn't let her. Sunnie remembered running back inside, through the back door. She remembered standing in the kitchen and suddenly realizing that "because I didn't share, I was going to hell."

Karin saw Sunnie's lip tremble, and then her eyes fill with tears as the emotional intensity rose again. Karin continued working with her, tapping, adjusting Reminder Phrases, until Sunnie calmed herself and suddenly came to the realization that she'd just been a little girl. Karin recognized that Sunnie was beginning to make the cognitive shift needed to change her perspective on this event and offered a reframe to encourage the natural shift.

Karin introduced a new question, "Would Jesus forgive that little girl?"

"Of course!" Sunnie said, her shoulders relaxing.

Karin's question helped Sunnie reframe the issue. Such reframes, asked when the intensity is three or below, can encourage clients toward making their own cognitive shift. Sunnie was able to move more quickly to the shift she naturally began on her own. Karin and Sunnie retested for intensity around the event and Sunnie reported the issue as completely resolved.

As Karin and Sunnie moved toward closing the session with more continuous tapping, Karin tested the results as she asked Sunnie if Jesus would be there at the gates of heaven. Sunnie started crying again, but this time she smiled through tears of relief. "Well, of course he will!"

When the session ended, Sunnie's face was brighter and more relaxed. She was no longer frightened to go outside or to drive home. Karin suggested that Sunnie had done a lot of great work, but she might be a bit tired, so perhaps her husband could do the driving one more time. This made Sunnie laugh and she said, "Sure."

As you can see, there can be many layers to a phobia. Some can be relieved in "one-minute wonders." Others, like Sunnie's, can be released in one thorough session. Frequently, however, *it takes multiple sessions to release a phobia*. Note that it was the consistent rapport and gentle questioning, using her natural human curiosity for clarification, that allowed Karin to open the door so that Sunnie herself could uncover the underlying issue and the core event.

Test Your Knowledge

1. True or false? When dealing with phobias deal with any high intensity around the fear before getting specific details about the phobia.

2. All of the following are good examples of a phobia, except
a. Mary is deathly afraid of spiders, no matter the size or type. She even experiences fear if she sees a photograph of a spider.
b. Jillian was involved in a terrible car accident as a teenager. Ever since then, she has been afraid to drive a car, and hasn't done so in over ten years.
c. On a mountain hike, Sue nearly steps on a rattlesnake. She experiences instant near-panic symptoms, gasping for breath, shaking, and, ultimately, running away.
d. Kelly refuses to take his small daughter to the local Party Place for her birthday because he feels sick whenever he sees the clown makeup the employees wear.

3. True or false? It is a good idea to test the client's level of phobic response in vivo before beginning to tap on the overall issue and its many aspects.

Answers can be found in Appendix E

Physical Issues

In the September 2003 issue of the NASW News (the publication of the National Association of Social Workers), Terry Altilio, the coordinator of social work in the department of pain medicine at Beth Israel Medical Center is quoted as saying, "[W]hen you talk to somebody about pain, you realize that only 15 percent is physical. The other 85 percent of suffering is psychosocial, spiritual, and existential." (O'Neil) Pain is not just a physical issue. Emotions play a large part. Felitti and colleagues (1998) explored the CDC's Adverse Childhood Experiences survey and found a correlation between traumatic experiences as a child and many of the most deadly and debilitating diseases of adulthood such as diabetes and heart disease.

You can see for yourself that physical issues have an emotional component, for example, in the way emotional stress leads to tension, usually tension in the muscles, and the way this tension aggravates pain. Likewise, "the body doesn't distinguish between physical and psychological threats. When you're stressed over a busy schedule, an argument with a friend, a traffic jam, or a mountain of bills, your body reacts just as strongly as if you were facing a life-or-death situation. If you have a lot of responsibilities and worries, your emergency stress

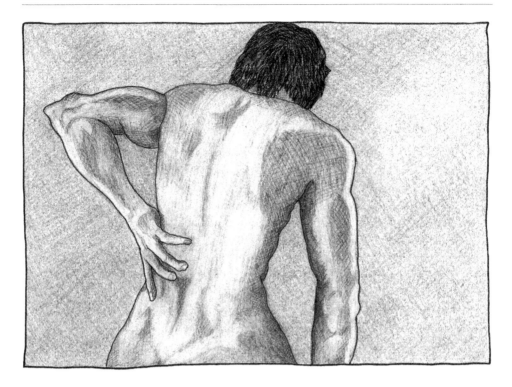

response may be "on" most of the time. The more your body's stress system is activated, the easier it is to turn on and the harder it is to shut off. Long-term exposure to stress can lead to serious health problems." (Smith, Jaffe-Gill, & Segal, 2010)

In our bodies, everything is connected to everything else. "Bodily functioning is a continuous adaptation process to our external and internal environments that is operated by the brain...Through these linkages, what is going on in our consciousness is continuously affecting our body – and vice versa." (Lincoln, 1991, p. 9) Physical pain reflects this connection. Since EFT balances the energy in the body, it can be successful in dealing with many aspects around pain, and often reduces the physical experience of pain. EFT demonstates the linkage between pain and emotions by addressing physical symptoms and emotional issues in exactly the same way. We cannot emphasize enough, however, that, legally and ethically, you must be very careful in the claims you make. Remember that, in certain locales, claiming to treat or cure physical issues or pain can be considered practicing medicine without a license. EFT "addresses energy imbalances in the body." It does not "treat" medical issues or pain.

That being said, let's move on to the use of EFT with physical concerns. In chapter 3 where we introduced Gentle Techniques, we used Chasing the Pain as a method for finding a physiological aspect to tap on when the emotion behind the physiological couldn't be articulated, either because the emotion was too intense or because the client was too disassociated from the emotion to talk about it. Chasing the Pain can also, of course, be used when the physiological is the presenting problem. Simply test its intensity, then follow the pain or discomfort wherever it seems to be in the body, tapping as you go.

Karin uses a variation of EFT developed by Paul Lynch called the "Color of Pain." There are many reasons a technique like this may be effective. The mechanisms behind trauma, disassociation, conscious, subconscious, physiology, metaphor, guided imagery, and EFT are undoubtedly quite complex. Although, it's beyond the scope of this coursebook to explore these ideas in detail, Appendix A offers some insights. Whatever the ultimate explanation for its effectiveness, the Color of Pain technique can be used to find or create specifics for use as EFT aspects. We know that EFT works best with specifics. The Color of Pain essentially turns a nebulous physiological reaction into an object that the mind can focus on more clearly.

Physical Issues Case Study – Dan

As this volume was being written, Karin demonstrated this technique during a level 2 EFT workshop with a participant who had come into the workshop saying he had long-term back pain that moved and changed but never seemed to go away. Having tried all sorts of therapies and techniques and visited a number of specialists, Dan was not only anxious about the pain but beginning to feel anger or resentment toward it as well. Dan was not sure he believed that anything could relieve it. The writing on his walls seemed to say that this meant something was really wrong with him.

Karin emphasized to the workshop observers that she would not mention the word "pain," nor would she talk about Dan's emotions or what had been happening in his life when the pain first began. Her goal for this demonstration was to turn the pain into an object with specific aspects that could be tapped on. Karin began by asking for the SUD level on the pain. Sitting it was a 6, but when standing it was a 9.5. She then began asking Dan questions about the pain as an object. If the pain had a color, what would it be? Texture? Size? Material? Movement? Sound? To help her form questions, Karin asked for clarifying details so that she, too, could imagine the object. She used the room's white board to write down the aspects as they were uncovered so that she, Dan, and the workshop participants could envision the object themselves and track any changes to the object as they tapped. Karin helped Dan refer to the pain as "it" and "this thing" to help him to "see" it as an object. Karin started to clarify specifics:

Karin: So this thing in your body, if it had a color, what would it be?

Dan: Umm, it's dark gray, almost black.

Karin: Is it solid, or ___?

Dan: It's... shadowy. Like a deep shadow.

Karin: Okay, this dark shadowy thing, how big is it? Is it moving?

Dan:	It's pretty big, bigger than my hand, and… like… wiggling, no, like undulating, like an amoeba.			

Karin: So, it's a big, dark, gray, undulating, shadowy amoeba. Is that right? Is it making any noise?

Dan nodded and laughed nervously, saying, "Yeah, it's sort of… hissing at me." She went on to gather as many details of this thing as possible. As Dan was already familiar with EFT's Basic Recipe, Karin began to tap on her own body, leading Dan to follow along with a specific Setup and a simple acceptance statement: "Even though, I have this big, dark, gray, undulating, shadowy, hissing amoeba, I'm okay right here, right now. Is that true? Are you okay right here right now?"

"Yes," Dan said, then followed, saying the Setup and tapping the points. Karin led Dan through the Basic Recipe a couple of times, stating the words Dan used to describe the object. She then stopped tapping, instructed Dan to close his eyes, and asked how the object had changed.

Karin: How has it changed? What color is it now? Is it still almost gray? Is it the same size? Smaller? Larger?

Dan: It's lighter gray, now, and not as heavy. And a little smaller. It moved over here, to the other side.

Karin: Okay, so it's on the other side. Is it still undulating, like an amoeba?

Dan: No, it's like… wavy. Like rippling. And it's playing with me, saying, "Catch me if you can."

Karin wrote the changes down next to the original descriptions. It became like a chart of changes.

bigger than hand	smaller than hand	quarter sized	dot	gone
dark gray	lighter gray	lighter	even lighter	
undulating amoeba	wavy	still moving	wiggling a little	
shadowy	still shadowy	lighter shadow	fuzzy, pale	
lower left side	right side	still shifting around	appearing and disappearing	
hissing	catch me if you can	said hi	quiet	

Karin: So, let's tap on these changes. Even though I have this amoeba in my back, now it's a lighter gray (tapping Top of the Head point) and it's waving (Eyebrow) and not undulating anymore (Side of Eye) and smaller than a hand (Under Eye), and it's saying, "Catch me if you can" (Collarbone), and it's playing games...

With each set of changes, Karin led Dan to tap on those specifics, starting with the Setup on the Karate Chop point and then changing points with each description of the thing used as a Reminder Phrase: "Even though it's a quarter-sized dot, lighter gray, still moving, disappears and appears, and says 'Catch me if you can,' I'm okay right here, right now." "Even though I have this dot now and it's no longer an amoeba and it was whispering but now it's disappearing..."

As Dan's object diminished and he and Karin finished a round of tapping, Karin asked how the object seemed at that point. Dan started, shifting his body, looking for the pain, then laughed. He was obviously amazed. "It's gone!" Dan felt his back with both hands, shifted his weight. "The pain is gone. I've tried so many things that didn't work and now it's gone!"

Karin led Dan in one last round of tapping: "Even though I had the thing and it said hi and it moved, and had all these changes, all these colors, and it was talking to me, and now it's not there anymore..."

 Test Your Knowledge

1. True or false? The sensation of pain moving around in the body is a common physiological response.

2. All of the following statements are true, except
a. Physical issues are often related to emotional events.
b. Clients need to see appropriate medical professionals even while using EFT.
c. EFT addresses energy imbalances in the body. It does not treat medical issues or pain.
d. It's okay to tell people that EFT cures physical issues.

3. True or false? Metaphor is useful in dealing with physiological reactions.

Answers can be found in Appendix E

Chapter 10 – Trap Doors

As people begin to address core issues and dispel old beliefs that have been limiting their lives, as they work through long-term issues like phobias or pain, many begin to look toward more proactive methods for exploring their "palaces." One of the most popular positive steps that people explore is the use of affirmations. We've all heard that positive thinking and affirmations can be powerful. Your consistent thoughts become your reality through the "law of attraction." There are many books, websites, and workshops that teach that if you consistently repeat statements such as "My natural normal weight is 125 and that is what I weigh" or "I make $100,000 a year easily and comfortably," you will attract these conditions into your life. After a while, you may start to wonder if I've been repeating this affirmation every morning and every night for a year, why am I still at 190 pounds and still struggling to make ends meet?

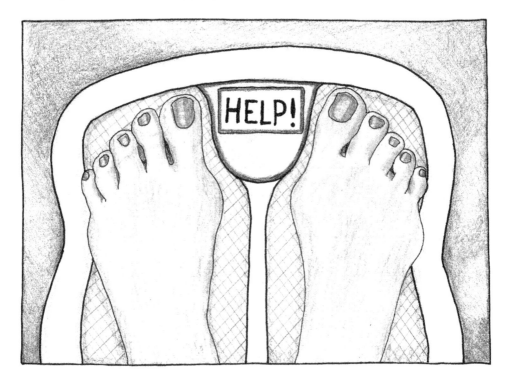

Craig (nda) explained in *The Palace of Possibilities: Using EFT to Achieve One's Potential* that the reason our affirmations don't seem to work is that we are not *actually* affirming what we *think* we are. What we are *actually* affirming is the writing on our walls. If that writing conflicts with our positive goals, we will not see the results we expect.

For example, you say to yourself in the bathroom mirror every morning, "I make $100,000 a year," but silently, even unconsciously, you think, "Only selfish people care about money." With every repetition of your affirmation you *reaffirm*

111

that limiting belief. As we attempt to explore our palace, entering new rooms, or trying new hallways, these hidden beliefs act like trapdoors we fall through to end up back where we started. Before affirmations can be successful, we must identify and eradicate these additional limiting beliefs. We do this by looking for what Craig called "tail-enders."

Tail-Enders

Tail-enders are the "yes, but" comments that follow a positive affirmation or statement of a goal. Affirmations are, by definition, statements that are contrary to the present situation, contrary to actual objective fact, because they are what we *say* we *want* to be true. The challenge in developing successful affirmations is that, although they are statements that we *say* we want, they are often contrary to what we *actually* think, feel, or believe. What we actually believe may manifest as "tail-enders," negating statements that, when identified, clearly show you the real "truth" of the matter, the "writing on your walls."

It's difficult to achieve a goal if you are limited by what you, even if only unconsciously, *know* to be *the way things really are.* These tail-enders can take persistence to find, but finding them is often productive as they lead you to core issues that can be neutralized with EFT.

Suppose a young woman wants to lose weight and states a goal, "I will lose ten pounds in the two months before my trip to the beach." If the affirmation is immediately followed by the thought "*Yes, but,* then I'll have to worry about men hitting on me," the belief that losing weight is somehow dangerous is reinforced. The writing on her walls may read, "I'll look slutty" or "Men only want one thing." Other possible "yes, buts" might be "I'll have to give up my favorite foods" or "If I go to all this trouble, I'll still be ugly and no one will want me anyway" or "This is too hard" or "I've tried it before and I gained it all back" or "I don't deserve to be thin" or "Who do you think you are to be thinner than your family?" There are infinite variations on these tail-enders or "yes, buts." Each can be turned into a specific Setup and addressed with tapping sequences.

Affirmations *do* work. They *can* help you succeed in meeting your goals, but only *after* your "yes, buts" are resolved. You must make sure that you are affirming what you *really* want to affirm. This means we must clear out the "yes, buts." This is where EFT comes in. EFT can rid us of the limiting writing on our walls so that we can take advantage of the power that affirmations have to build new beliefs. As Craig said, "erase and replace." (Craig, nda, p. 13). Combining the power of EFT to resolve tail-enders with the power of affirmations to create new beliefs is a powerful tool for creating positive change in our lives.

If your affirmations don't have the effect you want, but no tail-ender seems obvious, ask yourself what you might be overlooking. If you don't know, try just guessing or just pretend you know. Ask yourself, "If there *were* an emotional block keeping the affirmation from working, what would it be?" Write out your theory of what might be behind the issue, even if it seems you are just making it up; it is all relevant.

Whenever possible, break your tail-enders down into specific events. Ask yourself investigative questions. Who taught me that? Where did I learn this? What events in my life hold this limiting belief in place? How do I "prove" to myself that this is true? What do I do to reinforce this?

For example, Nora came to see Karin because she wanted to be healthy. She was always catching colds and getting stomach aches. Her doctors couldn't find a cause. Karin asked her to say out loud "I want to be healthy, but...." Nora finished the sentence with "my husband pays attention to me when I'm sick." Karin asked her when was the first time she could remember that someone paid attention to her when she was sick. Nora thought a moment and said, "Well, I had five brothers and sisters and I remember how nice it was when my mother took care of me when I was sick." Nora also expressed how silly it seemed to her that her mother caring for her could possibly affect her health. Karin explained tail-enders and limiting beliefs, and they began tapping with "Even though I want to be healthy, it was really nice when my mommy would take care of me when I was sick and I deeply and completely love and accept myself anyway."

Tap on each event you bring up until the intensity of your reaction is down to 0. Any event from your past that comes to mind is most likely related to where and how you developed your tail-ender, even if it doesn't, at first, appear to be related. Clearing *any* negative learning is always beneficial.

After using the Watch the Movie Technique or the Tell the Story technique to clear all events that come up, go back and check the "truth" of the tail-ender. (You might use the VOC scale for this.) If the negative belief still appears "true" in any way, look for other events that hold it in place. Remember you might find tables stacked on top of tables. Your goal is to neutralize any negative learning that prevents you from meeting your goal or realizing your affirmation.

After tapping for any tail-enders, review your affirmation. Is it still a clear statement of what you *really* want? You may realize you want more short-term goals, so, for instance, you might modify your weight goal to what you can do in just one month or you might adjust your goal. For instance, you may find that Weight Watchers meetings conflict with a spinning class you want to attend, so you decide to find an online Weight Watchers support group.

You may find that your goal is not really what you thought it was. For instance, suppose your goal was to increase your income by seeing two extra clients each week and you decided to find these clients by attending three community meetings per month. After meeting, following up, and collaborating with six new clients, you realize that your real interest, and their real need, is for sharing the information of your field. You realize your goal is not *primarily* money; rather, it is to share the insights you have gained over the years. You may decide to revise your goals to work with groups rather than finding individual clients. Revise your affirmation to reflect your new insights. Repeat your affirmation often, watch for further aspects or tail-enders that may develop, and tap whenever any objection comes up.

Note: For those familiar with EMDR (Eye Movement Desensitization and Reprocessing), you will recognize the concept of tail-enders as "tailgates."

Testing for Tail-Enders

When you think you have dealt with all the tail-enders that exist, test for the possibility that there may be additional hidden ones by imagining what will change in your life now that the limiting thoughts, feelings, and beliefs that you have expunged are finally gone. When you imagine life without these limiting issues, what do you see, hear, and feel? For example, suppose the tail-ender for your goal to network more to find new clients was that you have always been too shy to meet new people. Having tapped for this limiting belief and assuming that this tail-ender is gone, you attempt to vividly imagine your future without it. As you do, you notice physical symptoms of anxiety coming up. As you tap for these feelings, you remember the time when your brother wouldn't let you play basketball with him and his friends and how left out and lonely you felt. As you tap for these specific feelings and details around this event, you uncover the core issue of "If my own brother doesn't like me, I'm unlikable. I have nothing to offer others." You may be able to clear this issue once you recognize it, or you may find yourself surprised at its persistence. Remember, you can always get help dealing with a difficult core issue. We all need help sometimes, so call a tapping buddy or an EFT practitioner for help whenever needed.

Reversals

The concept of Psychological Reversals was introduced in level 1, but it is a common idea in energy work. Because reversals can be difficult to anticipate, Craig developed the Setup to preclude the necessity for diagnosing reversals. Even though reversals are relatively uncommon, Craig felt it was easier to always do the Setup than to test or wait for a reversal to show up. In EFT, a reversal of any type is usually dealt with by tapping the Karate Chop point or rubbing the Sore Spot in a circular motion while saying the "Even though" statement.

You will often recognize reversals by an apparent resistance to letting go of a problem. This resistance could be conscious or unconscious, the result of the writing on the walls or tail-enders. These beliefs and resistance tend to be protective in nature. Even many maladaptive behaviors were established early in life to protect us in some way. Although the behavior or belief may have been useful initially, these same behaviors or beliefs may now be inappropriate or holding us back from what we want. In such cases, the goal is to recognize and appreciate the intent of the resistance. In EFT, we work to *accept what is now* before we try to change it. This can take the form of creating a Setup such as "Even though part of me does not want to get over [the impact of this event], I deeply and completely accept all of me, including that part that resists getting over this because it wants to protect me in some way." Acceptance frees up the energy we spend rejecting those objectionable parts of ourselves.

Karin Davidson describes it this way to children: "You get mad at your teacher because maybe it hurts too much to think you are wrong or stupid. So you say thank you to that part that is mad so it feels better and then that part is glad to move on and feel even better by fixing the thing that made it mad in the first place. Thank you, mad part! I deeply and completely love and accept you for keeping me safe from feeling stupid. So now, mad part, how can we make it all better instead of just being mad?"

Other writing on the walls that may not be obviously protective may keep us from letting go. Fred Gallo (2000) described a set of criteria that encompass the types of beliefs behind many reversals. These criteria are often entwined and it is common to see one or more affecting the same issue. The set of criteria does not list every resistance that can prevent full utilization of EFT but gives you a place to start looking. These self-sabotaging beliefs that manifest as reversals are frequently based on identity, safety, concepts of deservedness, lack of perceived benefit, and others. Here are some of the factors and beliefs to look for:

- **Identity.** *I won't be me if I get over this.* To identify limiting beliefs of this type, listen for absolutes: always, never. "I've always been this way. This is who I am. I was born this way." Some limiting identity issues can be difficult to recognize on our own since we truly believe *this is truth*. Going back to our palace metaphor, we limit the rooms we explore, because we don't even *see* those rooms. As far as we are concerned, the rooms we live in are all there is. For example, "I've never been a good speaker so I could never teach EFT to others." If you are convinced of this truth, you may never consider addressing your identity beliefs with tapping because, after all, it's not a problem, it's a truth! It may never occur to you to ask what evidence there is for this. If it were true before, is it still true now? What experiences led to believing this? What is this belief protecting me from? Another example is "My life was ruined when my parents divorced." This person blamed the divorce for all bad things that happened in his life. The divorce defines this person's identity. It could feel threatening to suggest letting go of this belief.

- **Unwillingness to Forgive.** *If I forgive them, that means they got away with it.* Forgiveness is a sticky issue for many people, but remember that the goal of EFT is not to forgive. If you are working with someone who resists addressing an issue because she doesn't want to forgive someone, you can emphasize that the goal of EFT is to resolve the specific events and neutralize the emotions that hold negative beliefs in place. It is never necessary to "force" forgiveness on anyone. Once the emotions are neutralized and there is a natural welling up of peace and calm, this feeling may or may not include forgiveness.

- **Deprivation.** *I will be deprived if I get over this.* As Casey began tapping for the constant fatigue she felt, she realized she didn't want to change. Her illness was serving her well. Her spouse and children did much of the housework. A doctor's note let her leave work early on Fridays. She didn't think that her life would be better without the problem. On the contrary, she thought its resolution would deprive her of attention, sympathy, and help. She might have used EFT to explore the beliefs that made her feel she needed illness to get her needs met, but she elected, instead, to stop EFT.

- **Benefit.** *There is no benefit to me to getting over this.* Similar to issues of deprivation, this benefit could create another version of reversal: "I don't want to get over this. If I get over this, I'll lose the benefits of it."
- **Deservedness.** *I don't deserve to get over this.* One example of this can be tied to feelings of guilt and an inability to forgive yourself. "I'm guilty, so I don't deserve to get over this. I deserve to be punished this way."
- **Safety.** *It's not safe for me to get over this.* This issue might be related to being overprotected by an anxious parent or to present-day perceptions of risk. For example, Josey said, "It's not safe for me to look closely at my relationship with my husband. If I do, I'll probably have to leave him, but I can't take care of my children on my own."
- **Looping.** *I have to have [this] before I can do [that].* This is a perfect way to stay stuck and not make any progress toward any goal. Often the "*this*" is something totally out of the person's control, such as the reliance on the behavior of another person. "I can't be happy until my husband quits drinking."
- **Motivation.** *I won't do what is necessary to get over this.*
- **Possibility.** *It is not possible for me to get over this.*

Tapping for Reversals

Some practitioners emphasize reversals as an important concept to be addressed separately. Some simply look at any reversal as just another issue to work on. Much of EFT is still experimental and continues to develop, so different interpretations are inevitable. Whatever you decide about reversals, the concept of looking for resistance to letting go of a problem is a useful one.

It's common for all of us to fear the change or losses that may accompany letting go of old beliefs and issues. After all, if an issue has been part of your life for a long time, you have no idea what will happen if and when it is gone. When progress with EFT seems to slow or stall, look for what advantage holding on to the problem might have. What is the unconscious resistance to changing? What disadvantages are there to giving it up? What beliefs have protected you from these disadvantages in the past?

We all have "parts" of ourselves. One part may want to resolve the issue and another part may want to hang on to it because it is familiar or safe or whatever. This internal conflict can be uncomfortable. It may actually make good sense to explore the possibilities of what could happen if there were a change. At this point, you may not even be sure the issue *can* be resolved. You may be afraid it will be too painful. Perhaps you don't know what resolving this conflict will mean to your life. Or you don't yet know how changing your perceptions could change your life. Resisting change is human nature. *All changes, even the good ones, are stressful and can be a bit scary.*

Such conflicts may make it appear that EFT is not working for you. Working with conflicts uses the same concepts of asking investigative questions, developing a meaningful Setup, and tapping on the points. Modify the acceptance part of the Setup until the phrase feels true. In addition, you might tap for the actual conflict itself:

Even though part of me thinks _____, I deeply and completely accept all parts of me.

Even though part of me wants to keep _____, I deeply and completely accept this part of me and how it is trying to protect me.

Even though part of me wants to get over this and part of me wants to keep it, I deeply and completely accept all of myself, even the part that wants to hold on to this.

Even though I have this conflict between the part of me wanting to resolve this issue and the part of me wanting to keep it, I deeply and completely accept this conflict and completely accept that this is where I am right now.

Tap the points with the Reminder Phrase "this conflict" or use extended Reminder Phrases with reframing comments. Keep tapping points until you feel some shift or some other event or emotion comes up.

Eyebrow	My parts are in conflict.
Side of the eye	One part wants to get over this.
Under the eye	One part wants to keep it.
Under the nose	What a conflict!
Chin	One part wants to let go.
Collarbone	One part is protecting me.
Under arm	What a conflict.
Head point	I wonder how they will resolve this.
Eyebrow...	I wonder if there is an option that will make both parts happy.

Continue with the points and extended Setup until intensity lowers. Reassess intensity after each tapping. As necessary, look for additional aspects, develop new Setups, or tap more points. Be persistent, continuing until intensity is 0.

For practitioners, having clients who harbor a lot of resistance can be challenging. Unless the client can recognize the benefit to giving up an issue, which is not always easy to see, you can lose the client. Good rapport and client assessment is important. When a client's life is organized around her problems, go very slowly. Take baby steps. Find a very small issue to address first so that the client can build confidence in EFT and in you. Remember, it may actually make good sense to explore with your client the impact of changing.

118

Choices Method

Another technique for using EFT to reach goals and realize affirmations is to modify Setups and Reminder Phrases with Dr. Patricia Carrington's Choices Method. Before beginning to use EFT clinically, Dr. Carrington had already been helping her clients develop affirmations as a choice. Instead of the usual "I am [this]," the client would use "I *choose* [this]." She found that using a choice statement as an affirmation often circumvented self-sabotaging tail-enders. After all, it is often easier to accept a choice of your own making than to accept an affirmation you "know" is contrary to fact. As Craig (2008) wrote, in *EFT for Back Pain*, with the standard "type of Setup Phrase, you can tap a problem out. But Dr. Carrington took a different approach and showed that you can also tap a *solution* in" (p. 91). This method fits well with Craig's desire to use EFT to explore individual potential. The key difference between this method and standard EFT is that you work with the client to develop a compelling choice *prior* to developing Setups. Using a choice in place of the standard acceptance statement is, basically, a type of reframe, which clients develop themselves.

Choices can be a valuable addition to the tapping process. The use of Choices, however, is often misunderstood. Many practitioners tend to add the statement "I choose to ____" to the affirmation part of a Setup. Remember, though, that Choices is a type of reframe, so like other reframes it must not be added too early in the process. Remember, also, that this type of reframe must be made with the client's thoughtful participation. The Choices reframe is *not* a reframe the practitioner adds when she feels the client is ready. The client makes *all* of the decisions about what to choose and when. You may make suggestions of choices but the actual choice must be the client's.

In her eBook, *The Magic of Personal Choice in EFT: An Introduction to the EFT Choices Method,* Dr. Carrington offers criteria for making effective use of Choices. They are summarized here:

• **Be specific.** This is just as important a concept in the Choices Method as it is in standard EFT. Just as you are specific when you identify the negative, be as specific as possible when you identify the details of the positive choices.

• **Create "pulling" Choices.** Add words that will entice the mind, like I choose to "be surprised at___" or I choose to "find a creative way to___" The idea is to create a compelling choice that the mind will be happy to get on board with. Make your choice as attractive as possible.

• **Strive for the best possible outcome.** Take the time to help the client develop the exact right choice. Getting to the specific and accurate desired outcome is what makes Choices effective against tail-enders. Another way of thinking about this concept is to "ask for 100 percent of what you want." In other words, don't shortchange your choice before you've even tried for it.

• **State your Choices in the positive.** As you work to find the best outcome, you will find that many people know what they *don't* want but find it difficult to articulate what they *do* want. Sometimes this takes the form of a statement of what you don't like, such as "I want my boss to stop yelling at me," and sometimes it's just a comparison to the status quo, as in " I want a better car." Where possible, you want to give your literal mind a fully positive picture of your choice. "I want a job where I am respected and valued." "I want a current model Subaru."

- **Make Choices that apply to you.** EFT is not magic. All choices are *yours*. You cannot make choices for someone else, so choosing for your boss to stop yelling will not be helpful.
- **Make Choices that are easy to pronounce.** Use simple, short Choices while tapping. If, after being very specific and compelling and positive, you've created a couple of paragraphs, you may wish to write down your long version but create a shorter, more general version that encompasses all the ideas in your Choice. This will make your Choice easy to repeat.

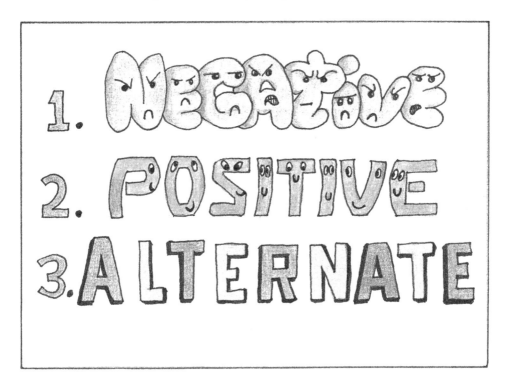

Using Choices with the Choices Trio

Once the choice is developed, start using Choices by assessing the intensity around the presenting problem, just as in standard EFT. How much does the issue bother you now? Begin the Setup with the standard "Even though" statement, being specific, but replace the acceptance statement with the Choice. For example, suppose you need to give a talk and you feel anxiety at an 8.

Begin tapping the Karate Chop point with the standard Setup ended with the Choice: "Even though I'm so scared that my stomach hurts because I have to talk in front of people, I choose to find it easy to give my talk calmly and with confidence so that giving my talk is interesting and fun."

Follow with three rounds of tapping, which is referred to as "the Choices Trio." (Dr. Carrington recommends the Basic Recipe for use with Choices.) For the first round of tapping, use the standard "negative" Reminder Phrase based on the problem "So scared my stomach hurts."

For the second round of the Trio, tap while saying the "positive" Choice at each point: "Choose to talk calmly and confidently."

For the third round of the Trio, alternate the negative and positive phrases, using the negative on the first point, the positive on the second, and so on. Always end on a positive, so add an extra point for this purpose if necessary.

As always, reassess intensity and, if needed, repeat the trio. Adjust phrases, tapping, and points as needed.

 Test Your Knowledge

1. True or false? It is important to consistently bring up the positive while tapping with a client because the client will begin to attract the desired results.

2. An example of a tail-ender for the positive goal "I will get to work on time every day by setting my alarm clock for twenty minutes earlier" is
a. "But I've said that before and it never works."
b. "Except Tuesday because traffic is not as bad on Tuesday."
c. "But it is important to get enough sleep so I don't feel cranky."
d. All of the above.

3. True or false? One way of addressing reversals is to recognize and appreciate the intent of the resistance.

4. Which of the following often underlie negative beliefs?
a. Deservedness
b. Safety
c. Benefit
d. Deprivation
e. All of the above

5. True or false? One effective way to test for remaining tail-enders is to try to imagine a positive future without the tail-ender.

Answers can be found in Appendix E

Lowering the Drawbridge

Perhaps now that we've learned EFT and begun to explore our own palaces, we might be ready to venture outside the palace walls. We can think of beginning to work with others as lowering the drawbridge, if you will, allowing others into our palaces or venturing forth to share theirs. Before we ride out on our trusty steeds, though, let's spend a little time in our own gardens. Before you begin seriously working with others, take stock of where you are with your own issues. As we've seen, it's important that you begin to understand the writing on your own walls so that clients' issues do not trigger you and you do not unknowingly push your values on clients. As Gwyneth Moss (ndb) says, "Maintenance of our emotional gardens is a process of weeding and planting and EFT is an ideal gardening tool."

Chapter 11 – Weeding Your Garden

Our first suggestion for weeding the garden is committed use of the Personal Peace Procedure. As you learned in level 1, this involves making a list of all your "issues" in life, breaking them down into specific events with all their aspects, differentiating tabletops from legs, then setting aside time each day to pick one item from your list, assess its intensity, and tap on it (along with any aspects around it that arise) until your intensity on the issue is 0. Some issues you'll finish in one tapping session, other issues may take several days. The key is to work consistently on your own issues, a little at a time.

Be persistent. Persistence is important. Although there are one- minute wonders in EFT, they are the exception. Most people are complex and have multiple layers to work through. Persistence is important when working with others, but it may be even more important when dealing with your own issues, because working on your own can be more challenging, especially when identity issues get in the way.

Sometimes it takes a while for the results of EFT to show up in your life, but you will begin to notice that you are reacting in different ways. You "forget" to buy the cookies you love so much; you roll your eyes rather than get angry when someone cuts in front of you; you talk to your mother calmly; you are able to ask effectively for what you want.

The reality is that the more of your own issues you resolve, the less you over-react, the calmer you are in the face of stressors. You are much less "triggered" by daily happenings. You are better able to see the broader picture in any situation, so you can make better decisions.

Keep it consistent. We humans seem to have a built-in ability to put things off until tomorrow. We procrastinate on just about everything, including tapping to release our old garbage. One way around this is to make an appointment with yourself. Put it in your calendar or diary and keep the appointment just as you would with anyone else. Another way is to tie tapping into a part of your daily routine. Tap in the bathroom or shower. Tap before lunch, dinner, or bed. What times would work best for you?

Keep it simple. Tap every time you have a negative emotion. Tap every time you have a physical pain. Tap when you catch yourself in nega-tive self-talk. Tap while reading an upsetting e-mail.

Ann's friend Mercedes had a job she hated. She felt sad, depressed, and trapped, with an empty feeling in her stomach. Ann taught her the Basic Recipe procedure and how to do a simple Setup. Mercedes decided she'd tap *every time she had that empty feeling in her stomach.* She called a few weeks later, saying that she still didn't love her job, but she recog-nized that there were some things about it she liked. She was much calmer and said she saw more choices and now had the energy to look for another job. Notice that Mercedes picked one specific feeling to tap for – *the empty feeling in her stomach* – that was indicative of her problem with her job. She kept her tapping simple and she was consistent. Do this for yourself. Help your clients do it as well. It is easy for them, and you, to feel overwhelmed if you try to do too much at once.

Shake it up a bit. Use some of the many tapping tips: tap in front of a mirror, tap looking at pictures, tap in the movies for a situation that hits close to you, sing the words as you tap, tap with both hands, tap each side with the opposite hand, tap listening to music that brings up emotion, tap while having an imaginary conversation with the people involved in your event, tap along with a tapping DVD, tap for the chocolate telling it how much you love it and hate it at the same time – be creative!

Deal with your resistance. Deal with any resistance to changing or addressing the issue by accepting the resistance. Go with it. "Even though there is no way I want to get over this and no one can make me, I deeply and completely accept myself. Even though I will keep all this 'stuff' because for some reason I need it, I deeply and completely accept my needs and my feelings. Even though I'm not sure I can get over all this even if I wanted to, I deeply and completely accept all of me including my insecurities."

Consult others. It is possible to work on our own stuff. Given that over one million EFT Manuals had been downloaded from Gary Craig's website by the time he retired, probably hundreds of thousands of people have worked on their own stuff. Working alone can be challenging because we don't want to go where we don't want to go. We sometimes don't even realize there is a problem. We all have blind spots that we don't realize need addressing. We have resistance or blocks or conflicts about changing: Who will I be? How will life change? How will life be different if I resolve these issues I've been carrying around for so long? Sometimes we need a little more knowledge and a few suggestions as to where to go next.

Janice was a beginning practitioner with a chronic physical issue. Chronic issues can be very difficult to address. Janice was determined to try to work on her issues herself but realized she needed direction. She made an appointment to see Ann because she wanted some suggestions as to what else she could try other than what she was doing. Janice had been diligent about tapping for the specific definition of her pain, with mild temporary relief, but got stuck with what else to do.

Ann gave her a list of ideas and exercises to try and Janice agreed that if she weren't making progress by the next week on her own, they would work on the issue together. Note here that Ann did not push Janice to tap with her. Janice's goal for the session was to learn more about how to use EFT for herself. She was not asking to work on her issues with Ann. Ann respected Janice's decision and where she was at the time. Assessing a client's readiness for tapping (or any technique for that matter) is important. You work with the client's timing, not your timing. It may take more than one session for a client to feel comfortable to work on more intimate issues.

Here's the list of ideas and things to try that Ann gave Janice, based on what Janice had told her:

• First, it's good to tap for the specific definition of your physical issue. Add in clarity as to *how* you know you actually have the problem. What are your emotions, how does this problem show up physically, what are your thoughts about it, who else would be affected by your resolving this, and what possible conflict could you have to resolving it?

• If you are not getting the results you want, assume a reversal or self-sabotage. Start each tapping session rubbing the Sore Spot while saying, "Even though part of me wants to hang on to this problem, I deeply and completely accept *all* of me, even that part that for whatever reason wants to hang on to this problem." Make a list of all possible benefits in your life to "holding on to this" and what belief you hold about yourself that could make this a benefit for you. This will lead you to core issues. Tap for each event that created any core belief. Somehow the problem fits the writing on your walls, your view of the world and yourself.

• Accept the problem itself: "Even though I may never get over this problem, I deeply and completely accept myself. Even though my body is not willing to let go of this yet, I deeply and completely accept my body/my life just as it is. Even though I am angry and don't accept my problem in any way, I accept myself, my problem and how I feel."

• Tap for related metaphors (such as for intestinal problems: having a gut full of ___, haven't got the guts to ___, I can't let go of ___, I'm holding on to ___, I'll feel empty if ___).

• What was going on in your life around the time this problem started? What was your family's history and reactions around this type of issue? Tap for any event that comes up, even if there is no conscious emotional reaction or you feel it is not related.

• Keep at it. When tapping on our own, we are prone to give up too soon. We have heard about the importance of persistence and we may use it with our clients. When working with ourselves, however, we tend to forget that some issues need lots of repetitive tapping.

Janice e-mailed Ann a week later saying she was now making progress. "It's funny," she wrote, "I've taken EFT classes and I actually knew to do all the things you suggested. Just having you listen and remind me was so helpful. Thanks."

Yes, it is "funny" that we don't use what we know for ourselves. It's another great way to sabotage our success. We could add that to our list of Setups:

Even though I am acting like I don't know what to do here, I deeply and completely accept myself and that I probably already know what I should do.

Even though I am blocking my own knowledge because for some reason I want to hang on to my issue, I accept that I am a fallible human being like everyone else in the world, with my own strengths and weaknesses.

Even though I have been to four EFT trainings and read at least six books and I can't figure out what to do for myself, I deeply and completely accept whatever is going on here.

Even though I can't seem to get out of my own way, I fully and deeply accept that is where I am right now.

Even though I know I'm a tough case, I also know that persistence really does pay off.

Now tap for whatever emotion or event or thought came up for you as you tapped for these statements.

Other Suggestions for Working Alone

Find a Tapping Buddy

Having a tapping buddy or seeking out an experienced EFT practitioner can be very beneficial in resolving your own issues. We often don't realize what our "stuff" is. We all have a deep need to be listened to and understood. Having that connection with another human is valuable. We often overlook even common questions and ways to use EFT. Having someone else explore your issues with you can make a big difference. An even stronger connection that can work in tough situations is to have someone else tap on you. Rapport and shared energetic connections are powerful.

Borrow Benefits

Another helpful method for dealing with your issues is to tap along with the many EFT tap-along articles, audiotapes and videos available, or a tape of your session with an EFT practitioner. Pick your issue, write down the intensity, then just tap along with whatever issue is being addressed by the EFT tap-along. This practice allows a mental disassociation that helps you get out of your own way and let your subconscious address what needs addressing. It also helps keep the work on your own issues interesting.

Notice Your Reactions to Events Now

We don't always remember our past events. We may have no immediate memory of the negative, even traumatic events that happen to us. One way to get in touch with issues that need addressing is to pay attention to how you react to events during the day. Do you have a stronger or different emotional reaction to the event than others around you? Do you later realize you overreacted to what happened? Have you received feedback from others who have no axe of their own to grind that you are reacting too strongly to what occurred? All of these are clues that point to unresolved past issues. Our interpretation of events, based on past experiences, triggers us in the present.

As children we learn ways of reacting to situations. At the time, these ways were designed to protect us or help us adapt to the world. After a few times of reacting in a particular way, our subconscious categorizes the behavior with the situation. We are always looking to make meaning of everything that happens. We tend to identify and categorize situations as similar situations that, in the real world, may not need the same intensity of reaction. The following are ways to help identify your own overreactions and help resolve past issues, balance your energy, and "recategorize" your responses.

Find similar situations

Think back to the last time you overreacted to a situation. Remember what you were thinking and feeling at the time? Now think of another couple of times in your recent past when you thought and felt the same way? What was happening then? What was similar about the events?

Can you remember an even earlier time you had these same feelings? How old were you? What was going on then? Do you remember what decision you made about yourself and the world then?

If you can't remember an earlier event yet, don't worry. Tap for your reaction to the current event. "Even though I got very angry when my coworker made a comment in the break room... Even though he wasn't talking about me and my reaction made me look silly in front of others, I deeply and completely accept myself and my reaction. Even though I can't remember any events *yet* that could have brought on such a strong reaction, I deeply and completely appreciate myself for starting to work on this problem."

Keep peeling

We often don't remember the very first time we reacted in a certain way; and if we do, we may not remember what decision we made about ourselves or the world. Tapping helps you remember. And if you still don't remember? Keep tapping for the triggers in the present time.

Be as descriptive as you can

"Even though my throat gets tight and I feel very afraid and think I must be doing something wrong whenever anyone looks at me sternly, and I don't remember where I learned this, I deeply and completely accept myself. Even though I feel depressed and start to cry and think I can't deal with the situation every time my boss tells me I made a mistake, and I don't know why I do this, I feel so silly..."

Tap for whatever clarity you have: how your body feels, your thoughts, your emotions. Tap for whatever past events do come up. Deal with all the aspects. Tap for any decisions you made at the time about yourself (any limiting beliefs) that came from the event(s).

Gwyneth Moss suggests you have a dialogue between your adult self and your child self. These "dialogues" are often useful to clarify how you came to believe what you believe and to explain to yourself why it is no longer necessary to carry this belief around. Tap while you are having this dialogue.

You can then also reframe what happened from an adult perspective. We make lots of decisions about the world and ourselves before we are six years old! We are still carrying around and operating from judgments made by a very young child. Look around at the children in your world who are six and under. Would you trust the advice they gave you? Would you make decisions based on their view of the world? Of course not, but that is exactly what many of us do. We are reacting as if we are still that child who learned that reaction.

Ask lots of questions to find out where this reaction was learned and then use EFT to resolve the events and release the negative learning.

Test Your Knowledge

1. *True or false?* If you are working on your own issues and get stuck, it is safe to assume there is a reversal or self-sabotage, and to look for the origin of the resistance.

2. *All of the following are true, except:*
a. When addressing your own issues, persistence is extremely important.
b. Sometimes we experience issues or blocks that require the help of an EFT professional.
c. The Personal Peace Procedure is a powerful tool for anyone working through his or her own issues.
d. It is important to learn to address your own issues, and tapping along with other aids or sessions will only hinder your ability to work effectively for yourself.

Answers can be found in Appendix E

Chapter 12 – Leaving the Palace

EFT is a powerful technique for working with emotional issues and, sooner or later, you will want to share that technique with others. There are a good many things to take into consideration as you begin to work with others using EFT. First and foremost, you must know the legalities for working with others that apply to you in your region and you *must* understand and adopt accepted ethical standards. If you decide to use EFT professionally, there will be many more considerations, because, at that point, you will be running a business. There are many sources for building and marketing successful businesses. For EFT, in particular, you may wish to consult Ann's book, *The Insider's Guide to Marketing Your EFT Practice*. The information it contains introduces you to some of the practical issues you need to consider when starting a business using EFT.

Working with Clients – Ethics

Being an ethical practitioner means more than asking a client if you may tap on her or sharing that EFT is still experimental. All licensed professional practitioners are subject to their profession's written code of ethics and are expected to act in an ethical manner. Organizations that recognize non-licensed EFT practitioners also have a written code of ethics, which members are expected to know and follow. Whether you are licensed or not, are you familiar with these guidelines?

What's the purpose of a code of ethics?

A code of ethics is meant to serve as a guideline for professional behavior. Primarily, the code is written to guide the decision making, behavior, and activities of the members in times when there might be a conflict or uncertainty. The code also provides a standard by which the public can hold the members accountable in the event of an ethical violation.

Does your code of ethics cover energy techniques?

Since ethical guidelines are updated occasionally, have you reviewed them recently? If you've practiced in other areas, we suggest you review these specifically from the perspective of practicing a new "unproven" modality. Since many professional codes of ethics were written prior to the advent of energy techniques, such as EFT, how does your code address using energy-based techniques? How does it address touching clients? Phone work? Does the code require insurance for all practitioners? Many insurance companies now cover energy techniques. Malpractice insurance is always a good idea, whether required or not. Risk management, or the activities you take to protect yourself from legal entanglements, is important for any business, and especially so for practitioners offering newer modalities such as EFT.

What are the rules in your area?

One of the common statements in a code of ethics has to do with your responsibility to follow the local rules, regulations, laws, and so on that apply to establishing a business in your geographic location. If you are taking money for services, for instance, a business license may be required. It is absolutely your responsibility to know the law where you live.

What is expected to be, or not be, stated in your marketing?

A code of ethics addresses marketing, but there are often governmental regulations concerning marketing as well. These will define what you may or may not call yourself and how you may advertise your services. Most codes state that you cannot offer guarantees of results.

If I'm not licensed, does any of this apply to me?

One of the purposes for an organizational code of ethics is to set up a standard by which the public can hold the members of that organization accountable.

Don't think, however, that if you are not a licensed professional and not a member of any organization, no such ethical standards apply to you. Governmental bodies are also "watchdogs" for the general public. In her article "Do You Have an Alternative Healing Practice? What I Discovered about How to Reduce Potential Legal Risks" (Hass, 2011), spiritual life path coach Rue Hass tells of her harrowing experience with Colorado's Department of Regulatory Agencies. While reviewing websites for problematic therapy-like language, the department targeted Hass's practice. Although the case was eventually dismissed and her name cleared, the cost in money, time, and stress was considerable. Find out what the regulatory guidelines are in your area.

Ethical decisions are not always simple.

A code of ethics often lists the core values behind the profession or organization. For example, the National Association of Social Workers (NASW) code of ethics, revised in 2008, lists the core values of service, social justice, dignity and worth of the person, importance of human relationships, integrity, and competence. The core values people hold often inform the decisions they make. These values are listed because it is never possible to write a complete set of "rules" to dictate behavior in all circumstances. For instance, the NASW code says, "There are many instances in social work where simple answers are not available to resolve complex ethical issues. Social workers should take into consideration all the values, principles, and standards in this Code that are relevant to any situation…"

Most codes make a broad statement about members' responsibility, not only to follow their profession's code, but also to learn about other resources and information that may be needed. The NASW, for instance, states this clearly:

> In addition to this Code, there are many other sources of information about ethical thinking that may be useful. Social workers should consider ethical theory and principles generally, social work theory and research, laws, regulations, agency policies, and other relevant codes of ethics, recognizing that among codes of ethics social workers should consider the NASW Code of Ethics as their primary source. Social workers also should be aware of the impact on ethical decision making of their clients' and their own personal values and cultural and religious beliefs and practices. They should be aware of any conflicts between personal and professional values and deal with them responsibly. For additional guidance social workers should consult the relevant literature on professional ethics and ethical decision making and seek appropriate consultation when faced with ethical dilemmas. This may involve consultation with an agency-based or social work organization's ethics committee, a regulatory body, knowledgeable colleagues, supervisors, or legal counsel.

What's the bottom line?

It is up to you, as a practitioner, to behave in an ethical manner to keep yourself and your client safe. It is up to you to be aware of any applicable professional or organizational codes, *and* applicable governmental regulations, *and* to be familiar with other relevant literature, theories, and research, *and* to seek consultation with others, including legal counsel if necessary, and (this is the most important point) to be aware of when any issue may become an "ethical" issue. It is up to you to interpret accurately what may or may not be ethical. Excellent resource for further study are David Feinstein's *Ethics Handbook for Energy Healing Practitioners* and *Creating Healing Relationships: Professional Standards for Energy Therapy Practitioners* by Dorothea Hover-Kramer.

Preframes – Introducing EFT

When introducing EFT to clients, it's helpful to create a "preframe" for this new experience. Ideally, by introducing EFT as similar to something the clients already know, you will help them fit this new experience into their existing frame of reference. People have a need to relate something new to something with which they are familiar. This new information is more easily accepted if you are able to tie EFT to a concept that is already well known.

We create categories in our minds, like filing cabinets, to hold similar experiences and knowledge. As EFT practitioners, we want to help others fit EFT into an existing category or "filing cabinet" in their heads. After all, it is much easier to put new information into an existing folder. By placing it in an existing folder, we are assimilating new knowledge into our existing system. This is much easier than creating a new system or changing the system to suit the new knowledge.

Recall Piaget's work with how people deal with new information. Most people prefer to assimilate the new into the familiar. The other option is to accommodate the information, which requires a paradigm shift and, as such, poses a bigger challenge. *It is easier to assimilate a new concept into what we already believe than to accommodate the new concept by changing our belief system.*

Make it simple

It is best to keep bridges, or preframes, simple. One of Ann's favorites is, "This technique calms you down so you can think more clearly about your problem." Encourage clients to experiment, "Let's see if this works for you." Another way to introduce EFT is to say, "I have a great technique that is getting terrific results. Would you like to try it?" This is positioning EFT as a technique that has worked for you and others in the past, and it is giving clients a choice. People like choices and they like to try things that have worked for others. Don't make anything up; be honest, even if you truly want them to try something. You should never try to push EFT on anyone.

You can also describe the benefits. Give people an idea of what's in it for them: "EFT often relieves the emotional impact of a negative event." Remember, you can also connect with what they do already by reminding them that comforting touches to the body, such as rubbing temples or wringing hands, are common everyday experiences.

The wonderful thing about EFT is that we can focus on an upsetting thought and, with intention, use touch or "tapping" on the body to transform the negative feeling into a neutral one. The reaction or emotion around that thought no longer "controls" us. We are no longer reactive.

As a licensed clinical social worker, Ann's preframe when working with mental health professionals is to refer to EFT as "a relaxation and calming technique, utilizing acupressure points, that modifies the anxiety response, fosters body awareness, and enables positive cognitive shifts." This statement touches on key results all therapists want for their clients.

How much to say?

Some people want a lot of scientific background on EFT; others want case studies showing success. Others only want to experience it for themselves. Some prefer to be given small bits of information at a time as they experience EFT for themselves; a minority want an entire explanation about EFT upfront. Adjust your preframe to the client's interest and needs, your own experiences with EFT, and your own style of delivery. The best EFT practitioners are good listeners. If you listen to what is important to your client, even in explaining EFT, you will connect better with them.

Note: Some professional codes of ethics require practitioners to tell all clients upfront that EFT is still an unproven technique. Check your guidelines as to what is mandated. But no matter how much or how little you share about EFT, the point here is to keep it simple and related to their level of interest and need. Some practitioners have clients sign a simple statement as part of their intake process and then ask if they have further questions.

It is sometimes difficult to know what to say. Creating a well-thought-out explanation ahead of time is helpful. Not only do you want a twenty-to-thirty-second introductory statement (sometimes called an "elevator speech"), but you want a couple of longer clear explanations as well. You want as smooth an explanation as possible to increase your credibility with your audience. You have several audiences, so plan several different introductions. None of these should be long. The explanation should spark interest and curiosity. Don't try to convince anyone. Relate and intrigue.

Preframes can also be used for specific emotional issues to give positive expectations of change. For example, EFT Master Jaqui Crooks (2006) has an effective preframe for those with anxiety.

She explains that negative patterns are set up in early childhood when we can't realistically assess whether those patterns will actually be useful over the long term. Our subconscious looks for patterns of reactions to daily events. This is helpful, as it keeps us from having to make a new decision every time something happens. So when, as a child, we respond to a few situations with anxiety, the subconscious sees this as a pattern and, from that time on, labels every similar event as one that should be responded to with anxiety. With this idea, you can see anxiety as just another habit or pattern, like biting your nails or always putting on your socks and shoes the same way.

As Crooks states in one of the handouts she uses for her classes:

137

One of the reasons you find it difficult to make the changes is because, if you do, the part [of your subconscious] that creates the anxiety will feel that it's redundant. It's worked hard all these years, doing the best it can for you, in the only way it knows how, and now, not only is it not being appreciated, it's going to lose the only job it knows how to do. Part of the work we will do is to explain to it that we appreciate what it's been doing, but we'd like it to do something different now. It's very obliging and it'll do that. (2006, p. 6)

Explaining this idea with this preframe helps your client see anxiety as something that can be addressed and relieved.

Getting Ready

Many practitioners take a few minutes before beginning a session with a client to tap for current stressors, to set intention, or to meditate just to relax and clear their own heads. You might tap for insecurities that come up in you about this client or tap to reach neutral emotions about seeing each client.

The following are important guidelines to keep in mind as you get ready.

Work without making assumptions

Because we create "categories" in our minds, we have a tendency to relate to a client issue with our own strategies and "writings on the walls." Keep in mind *that the meaning of an event to you is not the same as the meaning of a similar event to your client*. We all interpret events differently. Just because both you and your client experienced rejection by a boyfriend in high school, the death of a loved one, or some other trauma does not mean the event has the same meaning to both of you. It does not mean the client needs to address the same issues that you would.

You may both have felt rejection, grief, or loss, but the meaning of the event to each is different. *Never assume that the experience you had, the perception you had, the lessons you learned, or the decisions you made about yourself and the world are the same as your client's.* Even identical twins can experience the same event at the same time but have two completely different reactions. Don't assume. Explore what the event meant to the client.

Remain curious

If your client reminds you of someone you know, watch for the tendency to transfer your feelings about the other person to your client. Resist that all-too-human tendency to categorize or stereotype people. Remember, we put not only events, but also people in those categories in our head. *If you assume anything, assume that each client is different. Stay curious to find those differences.*

If things aren't moving as fast or as well as you'd like, relax. You just haven't gotten to the core issues yet. Be kind to yourself. EFT sessions are a two-way street. You do not have to be in control or fix things. Ask more questions. Stay curious.

Even the most experienced EFT practitioner runs into a blank. What do I do now? I don't know where to go or what to ask. Bring your focus back to the client and keep asking those investigative questions.

A very good question to ask in all situations in which you can't get to a core issue is "What am I missing here?" Sometimes the answer is found in putting together pieces of what the client has told you in a different way now, or focusing on something that, up to this point, seemed insignificant. Clients give clues, even when they don't know they are clues. Sometimes, however, what we are "missing" is *seeing our own role in the problem*. Doing your own work and getting consultation is invaluable. We all have our issues; we all have our blind spots. We are never 100 percent "done" with our issues.

Avoid pushing

You have seen EFT eliminate the negative emotions and limiting beliefs behind traumatic events. You know what's possible. However, never push clients to move faster than they are willing to go. Always work at their pace, not your pace. Like a guide dog, you make it safe for them to go down the road they choose, at the pace they choose. You don't choose the road. Your job is to provide safe passage. Do not push them to go faster or deeper.

Listen to your gut

As you work on your own issues, you become not only calmer, but also more intuitive and sensitive to your inner voice. You learn to trust and pay attention to what your gut tells you. Certainly, you want to clear any fear you have about working with clients, but do not work with people with whom you feel uneasy or uncomfortable. *You have no obligation to take on every client who calls. You are not responsible for dealing with everyone's problems.* When you ignore your intuition, you are inviting problems.

Building Rapport

EFT is more than tapping and talking at the same time. You want to learn something about your clients. It is important to require an intake. Ask relevant questions before you begin: What have they tried before? What's worked for them? What hasn't? What do they think is their biggest block/problem in life? What happened to bring them to see you now? What expectations do they have for EFT sessions? How will they know if their issue is resolved?

Assess how anxious a client is at the beginning of the session, even if the anxiety is about using this "strange" method. *Tapping to reduce current anxiety before beginning to address the issues that brought the client to you, helps the client relax and builds rapport.* Always develop positive rapport before getting into deeper issues.

Of course, if a client taps when truly tuned in to the event or emotion, EFT will work without deep rapport. Learning to develop excellent rapport with your clients, however, is a critical part of becoming a skilled practitioner. You need rapport for the client to feel comfortable enough to share negative feelings with you and to go into more painful events. A key responsibility for every practitioner is to create a safe and nonjudgmental environment. Feeling safe allows the client to address deeper issues and to find core issues. Core issues often involve looking at a negative self-image and, quite often, hidden shame and guilt, and your client must feel safe to share these events, thoughts, and feelings with you.

Keep in mind that your goal is to *minimize the level of intensity* around any emotional issue. Fortunately, with EFT, it is not necessary to discuss or emotionally relive the event to correct the energy disruption. The client needs only to feel safe enough to "tune in" to the disturbing event. A client can do this even without telling you about the situation. Your role is to ask questions to help find a specific event and more questions, if necessary, to clarify and make the event even more specific. Often, but not always, if you have good rapport with your client, after an issue is resolved, your client will share more personal details about the issue.

Common Questions from Clients

Common questions that clients ask practitioners are:

- *Can EFT really help?*
- *How much does it cost?*
- *How long does it take?*
- *What do I have to do?*
- *What do other people think of EFT?*
- *How long have you been doing EFT?*
- *What are your credentials?*
- *What results can I expect?*
- *How is EFT better than other methods?*
- *Are there any side effects?*
- *What are energy disruptions?*

You will find it helpful to think about your answers to such questions in advance. It's also helpful to develop answers to these questions when you are building your website.

Some clients may have read about EFT or have seen examples online and expect a "one-minute wonder." Although these do occur, they are the exception. There is no way to predict how sessions with any person will go or how long it will take. Let your client know that, generally, it takes a few sessions to find the core issues, but that most people feel some kind of relief with each session. This is a good preframe for the client. They can then watch for change as the sessions progress. Some clients will tell you they feel "different," more relaxed or less easily upset by day-to-day events. Often clients say that others around them noticed changes in their demeanor and behavior before they did.

Some clients may not give credit to the EFT work. This "apex effect" was first noted by Callahan (2002). He used the term to describe the tendency of some clients to give credit to any other reason besides tapping. Gwyneth Moss, EFT Master and AAMET trainer, likens it to going over a mountain. Once you get over the apex of the mountain, you can no longer see back to where you came from.

Potential Side Effects

Though few side effects have ever been reported, be sure clients understand the potential effects that energy work can elicit. Feeling tired after a session may be the most reported "side effect." Clients sometimes report feeling temporarily a bit fuzzy or nauseated. Other side effects could be tingling, feeling confused, or, conversely, feeling "wide open." These reactions can be reframed to the client as positive signs of change. When EFT clears a long-held reaction or emotion, it is possible to have some physical reaction. It's always good practice to ask clients how they feel before they leave your office (or before you disconnect from a phone/Internet session). If there is any side effect, you can then use EFT to balance the effect.

If clients experienced a great deal of trauma in relation to their issue or problem, you will want to proceed slowly. This may mean you don't attempt to eliminate everything in one session. Let them know, too, about the "peeling the onion" concept of dealing with one layer of their issues at a time. Warn them that this may lead to issues popping up between sessions.

Make sure your clients know the tapping points and routine well enough to tap on their own. Help them to develop a tapping routine for their life in between sessions. Sometimes what stops them is not being able to use the "right words" like their practitioner does. Remind them that simply tapping without words can be very useful when they are truly "tuned in" to their emotions or physical symptom. You might direct those wanting help in developing words for creating Setups and Reminder Phrases to sites like EFTwords.com.

Explain to clients that it's important to keep tapping if they do experience an emotional upset between sessions. For most issues that bring up emotions continuing to tap is important for full resolution. There is a difference, however, in experiencing strong emotions and "reliving" a traumatic event. If addressing a serious trauma tends to lead to reliving it, then *stop*. Don't push to the point of reliving trauma. Direct clients to do the same: Stop. Do something totally distracting – take a walk, play with the dog, call a friend. Practice the Constricted Breathing Technique throughout the day. Then work on much less intense issues.

Resolving any issue is helpful. As a practitioner, know when to use distancing or gentle techniques. If there has been stress in dealing with an issue, rather than going back to the trauma, start by addressing the fear of the fear of tuning in to the trauma. Do not tune in directly to the event itself until the fear of addressing the issue is at 3 or lower.

Some therapists encourage clients with high degrees of trauma to keep in touch by e-mail; some even give clients working through serious trauma a cell phone number to call. Be careful with such practices, however, that you, the practitioner, do not create an unhealthy dependence or cross healthy boundaries in your client relationships. You should never become a crutch for your clients. Encourage them to utilize EFT on their own so that the power of change is literally in their own hands. And as always, remind them that EFT is not a substitute for professional mental health care or medical assistance. Remember, too, to operate within your scope of practice and experience. If you have no experience or training in dealing with people with serious trauma, don't. Develop referral sources. Such sources often develop into reciprocal relationships.

Energy Disruptions

Some of your clients may want to know more about the concept of energy disruptions. Giving a simple explanation is a good place to start.

Our bodies have measurable energy. Medical tests such as EKGs and EEGs measure it. Lines of energy, or meridians, run through our bodies. These meridians have points that acupuncturists use to treat physical symptoms. In recent years, the energy on these meridian points has been measured. This energy can be disrupted in a variety of ways. EFT is based on the premise that our thoughts create disruptions – that it is our thoughts about an event that causes our energy system to be disrupted. EFT works to balance the energy disruption.

In MRI studies, the stimulation of acupoints has been shown to send signals directly to the fear-management limbic system of the brain. EFT studies performed over the last decade have shown that tapping relieves stress. Research by Carnegie Mellon University psychologist Sheldon Cohen shows that stress is a contributing factor in human disease, and in particular for depression, cardiovascular disease, and speeding the progression of HIV/AIDS (ScienceDaily, 2007).

Candace Pert (1999) pointed out in her book *Molecules of Emotion* that any change in the emotional state is accompanied by a change in our physiological state and that our memories are carried in the body, not just the brain. Three other helpful books about the mind-body connection and the influence of trauma are *The Body Bears the Burden*, by Robert Scaer; *Waking the Tiger*, by Peter Levine; and *The Body Remembers*, by Babette Rothschild.

EFT works on the premise that an imbalance in our energy system is causing our current emotional upset. The goal is to balance the energy. The Discovery Statement says: "The cause of all negative emotions is a disturbance in the body's energy system." This means that we are not upset because of what happened to us. We had a thought about the event, and the thought about it then disrupted our energy system and created the upset. If we balance the energy system, we also impact the thought that created the disruption. The emotional impact of the thought and the event is released by the tapping.

Using EFT, we work to identify which negative event created the negative belief that created the energetic imbalance that underlies the emotional upset.

Chapter 13 – Working with Special Populations

Phone Work

Although using EFT over the phone is introduced in level 2, many concepts that make a good phone EFT practitioner are detailed in level 3. We introduce the concept here because, as you work to tune into your client by phone, you begin to realize the importance of truly listening, connecting, getting out of your own way, and more.

The Upside

There are many benefits to phone work: You don't have to rent an office. Clients don't have to travel. You have flexible hours. Lack of mobility is not an issue. You can work in whatever comfortable clothes you choose. Some client problems, such as agoraphobia, can be addressed with less complexity. The very shy, very embarrassed, or shamed person has fewer barriers to getting start-ed. You don't have to worry about privacy issues of having one client leave before the other arrives. When you're limited to a narrow geographic area, you may need to treat a larger range of issues in order to attract enough clients. It can be difficult to focus on a specialty. Phone work and internet marketing allows you to develop your specialty and market to only those potential clients that need your particular skills.

The Downside

Although you can gather the same background information about people whether you see them face-to-face or over the phone, you can miss the subtle information communicated in how they walk into your office, facial expressions, posture, and so on. Webcams on computers help, but it's not quite the same. When doing phone work, you can't fully judge a client's level of vulnerability and sensitivity, which might affect the speed at which you move into issues. Without a camera, you can tell people where to tap but can't be sure they are doing it correctly. If they abreact, you can't tap on them or ensure they keep tapping. You don't know what support system they might have if needed, or if they are truly in a safe place for the session. If their emotions become intense, they may try to stop or hang up, and you can't help them to, either, keep tapping, or to shift their focus to the present (i.e. break state) to lessen the reactions.

It is always better to err on the side of caution. Yes, you are excited when clients call you. Yes, you may need the income. But stop and listen to your gut. If someone is very vulnerable or possibly may become extremely upset, it is better not to accept that person as a phone client. It is better for you, and better for the caller. Some people simply need more support than you can give over the phone. Help callers like this find a therapist in their local area.

Certain prescreening questions can help you make these decisions: What causes you to become very upset? How do you deal with being very upset? Who in your life do you consider supportive? Have you been given a mental health diagnosis? Are you currently taking medication for emotional problems?

Have a plan for what to do in case a client hangs up on you while in emotional distress. Have a policy in place about how you will handle this or discuss this possibility with the client as part of the intake process. Practitioners might choose to ask for a second phone number and an emergency contact phone number as part of the intake process.

Remember, don't go where you are not comfortable or not qualified.

Phone Work Basics

Once you've decided to accept a client over the phone, spend time getting to know her. Help the client clarify what she wants and why she has decided to deal with it now. Ask what has worked in the past. Ask how she knows she has the problem. Ask how she would know if she *didn't* have the presenting problem. This gives you a good idea of the client's long-term goals. Ask questions until you fully understand the client's situation and goals for her sessions with you.

Phone work is easier if both you and your client have a hands-free phone system. Set up your location to prevent interruptions. You will want to have a dedicated phone line without call waiting, or turn off this feature. As a practitioner, you want to ensure the area you will be using is quiet, without any distractions, barking dogs, or other interruptions by anyone in the house.

You will need to teach your phone clients where to tap. Some therapists e-mail a diagram of the points in advance or suggest that clients watch an online video to become familiar with the process and the points. Other practitioners carefully describe each point to their clients on the call as they believe clients should not be distracted by a piece of paper and that the client should give their full attention to what is happening during the phone session. Whatever you do, be very clear and simple in explanations and when defining the tapping points. It may be helpful, as you are describing the points, to tap them yourself as you go to help keep *you* focused. Remind your clients that if they don't fully understand or follow what you are doing to stop you and ask you to repeat the instructions. Ann likes to make sure clients know the points by having them describe back to her where they are tapping.

Phone work requires that you turn down your other senses and turn up your listening and intuitive skills. You will develop an increased ability to listen, not only to words, but also to all the subtle nuances of expression, such as tone, breath, and pauses. You may need to close your eyes, at least at first, to be truly able to tune in. Sometimes, even with lots of experience, you'll still want to close your eyes to focus when the session raises issues that are complex or very intense.

Test Your Knowledge

1. True or false? It is important to consider both the positive and negative elements of using EFT over the phone before accepting a phone client.

2. When working on the phone:
a. You cannot expect the same level of results as you would from an in-person session.
b. The space in which you are working has no effect on the session, since the client is not there.
c. You need to pay closer attention to things like verbal clues, changes in vocal levels, and even your own intuition.
d. All of the above.

Answers can be found in Appendix E

Working with Groups

Whenever possible, know your audience. Research each group to learn what you can. What is the group's interest and purpose? You want to present information in a way that will connect to the group. Some people just want to learn to drive the car; others want to learn how the engine is built. Address the needs of your audience. Though there are certainly similarities, how you go about building bridges to understanding, giving examples, and conducting exercises and how you help individuals have their own "aha" experience varies with the background, previous knowledge, and experiences of the group. When you are unsure of the background of the group, choose the most conservative approach. All types of groups can use EFT, but their way of learning and the way you present may be different.

Build your confidence by starting with groups with which you are familiar. If you're a Reiki master, start with others involved in Reiki. If you're a massage therapist, start with other massage therapists.

Borrowing Benefits in a Group

Borrowing Benefits is simply a means of working with a group by which everyone benefits from tapping along as they watch another person. Although you, as the leader, can tap without a "subject" on any chosen issue, Borrowing

147

Benefits is ordinarily conducted by focusing on one or more individuals in front of the group. The individuals demonstrating tap in front of the observers. The observers note, then set aside, issues of their own as they "borrow the benefit" of the demonstrators' tapping. Although this section discusses using Borrowing Benefits in a group setting, this method can be used in working alone, as an individual can tap along with any workshop or DVD session.

In the EFT Intermediate Library "Tutorial #10: Conducting a Borrowing Benefits Group," Craig writes, "After you have been practicing EFT with clients for a couple of years, and have developed solid Intermediate Level skills, you are ready to provide those benefits to clients in a group... Your role in a Borrowing Benefits group is twofold. Conduct the best session you can on one individual with all of the skills you have developed, and stop at appropriate intervals to be sure the group is following the instructions." (Craig, 2008f)

The participants do not need to understand EFT; they just need to tap as they follow along. The group leader need not be teaching or describing what is happening in the session (although when using Borrowing Benefits in an EFT class, it is helpful to stop and explain what you are doing). One explanation as to how Borrowing Benefits works is that the subconscious mind makes correlations with the demonstration and brings up the appropriate pieces to allow tapping to work on the identified issue. You might wish to introduce the concept of Borrowing Benefits by sharing stories of your successful experiences.

The leader begins by asking everyone in the group to identify a particular event to address. Spend time helping participants identify single specific events. The issue should be specific and measurable on an intensity scale. Suggest appropriate issues, such as nervousness about a future event, an embarrassing moment in the past, a specific dislike of a specific person, a specific physical feeling, or a recent source of irritation.

Ask them to give their event, aspect, or feeling a name and to write it down. If necessary, explain the intensity rating, then go on to have them assess their emotional intensity around the event and write that down next to the name.

Then instruct them to set this information aside and simply tap along with the demonstration, regardless of the issue being addressed in the demonstration. Tell them not to pay attention to their issue at all, but, instead, to focus on the demonstration (or video or audio demonstration).The beauty of Borrowing Benefits is that, even though the subject matter addressed by the practitioner in the demonstration may not relate to any other issues in the group, all group members generally experience a decrease in intensity around their chosen event.

Before beginning to tap, ensure that the group participants know the tapping points and are able to follow along. Conduct your live demonstration or play audio or video, as you would normally. Whenever you stop to check the intensity level within the demonstration, ask the audience members to check their intensity levels as well. Remind them to go back to the same exact event they started working on, as it is possible they may have switched aspects during tapping. Ask them to write down the new intensity. At the end of the session, have the participants check their intensity levels once again. Ask for a show of hands for numbers that went down by three or more points, and ask how many went to 0. If the group is small, go around the room asking people to call out their before and after numbers.

Note: As always, it is possible that someone in the group might have a strong emotional reaction. Many trainers have emotional assistants for this purpose. If you begin to run group sessions, keep this in mind and be prepared. At times, you may need to tap with the audience for their reaction to the demonstration they just watched.

 Test Your Knowledge

1. *True or false?* When Borrowing Benefits, as long as the observers tap along, it's not important that they tap on the same issue as the person they are watching.

2. *When demonstrating Borrowing Benefits, the presenter should do all except:*
a. Conduct the best session possible for the volunteer, calling on any needed EFT tools.
b. Make sure everyone assesses intensity before beginning.
c. Ensure that the members of the audience are emotionally connected to the demonstration.
d. Check occasionally to make sure the audience is tapping along.

Answers can be found in Appendix E

Children

Children usually love EFT. They are used to learning new things, so it does not seem unusual or strange to them. In working with children, keep Setups really simple; as with any client, use their own words. If they are obviously upset, just tap without words. Small children may find it helpful to spread their hands to show the amount of intensity in their problem. Older children do fine with the 0-10 intensity scale.

When working with children, Ann asks the child to shake hands and points out the spot where one person's fingers touch the other person's hand. She then introduces the Karate Chop spot as our "friendly spot" where we make friends with our problem. As a general rule, boys do as well as girls in using EFT. For some highly rational children, it may help to frame the concept of identifying emotions and physical feelings as a puzzle to solve. EFT can help them find and fit together all the pieces to the puzzle.

Some kids just don't "get" why you want to talk about such things as feelings and bad things that happened. Their strategy is to not look at it, not talk about it, and it will go away. They believe that talking about it is like reopening a wound. It will hurt. It may be easier for some to identify the physical representation of the emotion rather than the emotion itself. Ann explains to the child that when we have a feeling (emotion), we always have a physical feeling in our bodies as well. This physical response is the only way we know we have a feeling.

Sometimes, too, adolescent males balk at the affirmation part of the Setup. Find a phrase acceptable to them. There are suggestions are in the "Working with Children" handouts in Appendix C.

Most children enjoy making a movie of their story. Ask how long their movie is. Help them be specific by asking them to check out all five senses: what did they see, hear, feel, smell, or taste? Keep in mind that they don't have to tell you their story for EFT to be effective. Some children can't wait to tell you what is going on if you are truly interested and listening. Others don't want to share what happened, especially at first. That's okay. "Working in the Dark," as Ann calls tapping without the practitioner knowing the issue, can be a powerful alternative. Using questions about the submodalities can help you track their progress. Did the colors change? Did the problem get closer or further away? Is it louder or softer? Does it still smell or taste the same? Do you still feel it in the same place in your body?

In addition, these ideas work well with children:

- Blowing up balloons and releasing them as a metaphor for letting go of bad feelings.
- Making it a game.
- Saying the Setup for the child.
- Sitting a small child in a parent's lap and having the parent tap for the child as the parent tells the story.
- Having a parent tap on the child.
- Having a child tap without words, just focusing on the physical feeling.
- Tapping just for the number the child gives you (e.g., "This 8 in my stomach").
- Telling stories and tapping for fictional children who have similar problems as the child's.
- Tapping on a stuffed animal or puppet as a surrogate.
- Tapping on yourself as if you were the child to encourage them to tap along.
- Whispering the problem to a stuffed animal and tapping for that "secret."

To create ownership and commitment after teaching EFT to a child, let them name the EFT process, for example, "Lisa's Anger Solution" of "Tommy's Tapping." Instead of giving them a preprinted handout, have them draw a picture of the points on a figure or in a coloring book or write out the process for themselves. When possible, let them teach another person how to tap.

Tap for your own emotional reactions to or about the child, especially when working with cases of severe trauma. Working with children who have been traumatized can be draining for the practitioner. What some adults are capable of doing to children can be shocking. Be sure you take care of yourself. Tap for any secondary trauma for yourself. The more neutral and calm you are, the better you can listen and help. Children can be very sensitive, at times hypervigilant to the emotions of the adults around them. This is another good reason to work on your own issues. The stories our clients tell us can trigger our own issues, and children are experts at triggering adults!

Animals

Animals, like people, have a meridian system. Like people, animals have energy imbalances. Though it is possible to tap on some animals, other animals don't like to be touched at the location of the meridian points. Some can't be safely touched. There are EFT practitioners who actually tap on animals whenever possible and there are others who use only surrogate tapping for the animal. Both can be useful in dealing with animal issues.

Start by tapping for your own feelings around the animal's behavior. Clear your own energy around the problem so you can address the animal's issue from a neutral position.

Gwyneth Moss (nda) suggests that you address the Setup and tap from different perspectives when tapping for an animal:

• First, address the Setup and tapping *as if you are talking* about *the animal:* "Even though Spot shakes in thunderstorms, he is still a very good dog."

• Second, word the Setup and tapping *as if you are talking to the animal:* "Even though I notice that you act terrified any time there is thunder, I think you are a wonderful companion to me."

• Third, word the Setup and tapping *as if you are the animal:* "Even though I am scared of thunder, I am still a great companion."

Clarify, as specifically as possible, what it is you want to resolve. Whether surrogate tapping for an animal or another person, when you calm your internal chatter and truly tune in, it can be surprising how connected you can feel to the person or animal. Use whatever comes to mind as aspects, events, thoughts, or pictures in your head about the animal and what he is, or could have been, experiencing. Don't worry about being right. Continue tapping until no further aspects come to you and you feel the issue is completed.

Surrogate Tapping

The practice of surrogate tapping is tied to the concept that we are all energetically connected. Assuming this connection, when you focus your attention on other people, or animals, you connect with their energy systems. When we are truly able to get out of our own way and tune in to another person, we can tap as if we were that other person. Surrogate tapping enables the other person to benefit from the tapping you are doing on yourself. However unlikely this seems, when you focus on a specific aspect of any other living being's energy system and tap for that aspect, *as if you were that person or being,* you will see changes in that being's energy system.

Surrogate tapping can be challenging when tapping for someone close to you. Often you may be tapping for someone whose behavior is a problem to you. When tapping for "Even though Johnny shouts and yells, he is still a good kid," you may really be tapping for your goal. *You* want him to stop the noise, or stop yelling at *you.* It is important to *clear your own emotions and feelings around the problem behavior or issue before you surrogate tap for someone else.* Tap for your own feelings first, otherwise you will be tapping for your own agenda. If you are tapping for your own agenda, rarely will you see the results you would like. Surrogate tapping needs to be done from a neutral position. Of course, you *care* about helping the other person, but for the most effective results, you are not attached to the outcome. You can accept that what is, is.

Practitioners have developed various protocols for surrogate tapping, but the basic process is the same as for any other tapping. The difference is that you need to clear your associated emotions around the issue first and to be in a place where you can be quiet and focus your attention on the other. Say the Setups as if you were the other person. For example, if you are tapping to help a friend get over a breakup, you could say, "Even though I'm so hurt that Sam left me, I deeply and completely accept myself."

It is surprising how connected you can feel to the other person when you get out of your own way and truly focus on the other. Because of this, most practitioners recommend that at the end of a surrogate tapping session you tap a couple of rounds to reground yourself. For example, "Even though my energy has been focused on helping Sarah, I choose now to reground myself as me. I'm [*your name*]."

Test Your Knowledge

1. *True or false?* When tapping for an animal or working with a surrogate, it is important to first clear your own issues around the event or situation.

2. *The following is a good example of making EFT accessible to children:*
a. Having children use an alternative intensity measurement, such as spreading their hands apart to show intensity level.
b. Allowing children to draw their own picture of the tapping points on a figure.
c. Finding an affirmation phrase that is acceptable to the child or adolescent with whom you're working.
d. All of the above.

3. *True or false?* When working with children, it's important to first work on your own responses to the child's situaion in order to more effectively help the child work through his or her own emotions.

Answers can be found in Appendix E

Chapter 14 – Continuing the Journey

Once you have established an EFT practice, your skills will continually grow and increase as you work with clients. There are a number of other steps you can also take to facilitate your search for excellence.

In the book *EFT and Beyond: Cutting Edge Techniques for Personal Transformation,* editor John Bullough (2009) discusses the factors that various studies suggest make for an effective counselor. The behavior that makes the most difference is that the counselor or therapist consistently reaches for an objective just beyond his or her level of proficiency.

Increase your basic knowledge base

What level of training besides EFT do you have in working with others? If you have no educational background in counseling or coaching, we suggest you gain knowledge about communication and listening skills, creating rapport, ethics, and calibration skills. We also recommend a basic knowledge of NLP techniques. In-depth coverage of these related topics is beyond the scope of this volume.

Increase your training

Yes, you can learn EFT from a book or DVDs. Thousands have, but to have the opportunity to practice with feedback and to ask clarifying questions about points that are still unclear to you is invaluable. We encourage you to take a class from an experienced EFT trainer. We encourage you to go beyond level 2 to one or more level 3 classes and other EFT topics.

Increase your experience

If you have a current related professional practice, start by using EFT with your clients on anxiety issues or cravings, or use the Constricted Breathing Technique as a calming technique. Constricted breathing is a great way to introduce clients to EFT. Then move on to using it for phobias and more current issues that appear to be simple. EFT is a wonderful tool in calming upset clients to get them able to access the reasoning behind the emotion. As you become more comfortable with EFT, you can expand its use.

Practice, but be judicious in offering EFT

Family, friends, neighbors, coworkers, even strangers, are possible subjects and may allow you to practice EFT with them, at least for a single issue or for pain relief. Some may be willing to go further. Others will be reluctant to open up in ways useful for getting to core issues with EFT. They may be willing to let you show them how it works, but then hesitant to let you get more intimately involved in their lives. Working with someone's emotional issues is, after all, a big responsibility. Respect their decisions and don't push even when you feel sure EFT could help.

When you are first introduced to EFT, it is natural to get excited about something that can relieve the impact of negative experiences. Ann certainly was! Ann said when she first learned about EFT, she not only wanted to "try it on everything," but she also wanted to try it on *everyone*.

"If you had been within ten feet of me in the first few weeks, I'd have you tapping on something," she recalls. "I am afraid I was a bit obnoxious. My friends teased me that 'no one was safe' from my passionate sharing of EFT."

Passion can be a great motivator to make changes in the world, but (a caution here) keep your enthusiasm within reason. It is important to respect where the others around you are in their pursuit of their personal growth.

Karin often used EFT as an "emotional 911 response." When coworkers, employees, or family got very upset, she'd say, "I can help you feel better with this thing I found; may I hold your hand?" And she'd tap on their Karate Chop and finger points. People would consistently feel better and ask, "What the heck was that?"

Getting experience can be a challenge if you are just learning. You can get quite a lot of practice by working on your own issues. You can learn a lot by going to an experienced EFT practitioner for your stubborn issues. An EFT class is a great place to find a tapping buddy or to join a tapping group. Tapping regularly with others on your own issues can be very helpful. As you become more confident and practiced, volunteering at community programs is another option for getting practice. Finding people willing to "practice" tapping with you is much more about finding out where they want help in their life than it is selling them on EFT.

Most, if not all of us, listen to the station WIFM – *What's in It For Me*. People tune in to messages that resonate with their current issues of concern. Finding volunteers is a lot like finding clients. The focus is on the relationship. To let you tap with them, people need to know you on some level, like you in some way, and trust you to have their best interests in mind.

Continue to work on your own personal emotional issues

We all have blind spots. We all have issues. The more work you have done on yourself, the better practitioner you will be. The fewer of your own issues you have, the more credible you will be as a practitioner. Finding the right tapping buddy helps a lot, both in working on your own issues, and practicing EFT with another person long-term. As mentioned, EFT classes are great places to find a tapping buddy. Take responsibility for your own safety and healing when working with a tapping buddy (or for that matter, any EFT practitioner.) Just because someone attends an EFT class does not make them an expert for your issues.

When you find a tapping buddy, establish some ground rules to make the process most beneficial for both of you. Decide when, how often, how long, and for what period of time you are contracting for joint tapping sessions. Decide on an exit strategy as well. For best results, you need to be open and willing to share feelings and painful events. Generally, you can walk each other through whatever issue comes up. If, at any point, you feel your buddy cannot handle your issue, stop and seek a more experienced EFT practitioner. Take responsibility for your own well-being.

Ask for feedback

Seek consistent feedback on your performance as an EFT practitioner. Becoming a highly skilled practitioner means checking every session to see how the client feels about you and the work you are doing together. Tell clients you are interested in their assessment of your work together so that your future sessions can focus on what is best for them. You might want to explore such topics as: what they felt worked best in the session, what they would change, what should the focus be for next visit, and what they learned in the session. However you ask it, seek feedback as to your performance. Often, people are uncomfortable pointing out any negatives. Karin suggests that, at the very least, you ask for one positive thing you did well so you can keep doing it, and one thing that could be improved. This makes it more comfortable for your tapping buddy or client to give you feedback. However you do it, keep reaching for that next step in excellence.

Find a mentor/consultant

Having a mentor or consultant can be helpful in seeking feedback and reaching for that next step as well. The best therapists have a relationship, often a formal business contract, with another highly experienced person as a consultant or mentor. These therapists, in search of their own excellence, use their mentor/consultant to share problems, to generate ideas, and to access another perspective on their approaches with clients. When working with a mentor/consultant, the goal is to improve your own performance. The more open you are about your challenges, the more effective you will be in keeping your own issues out of the session and the more you will increase your ability to handle whatever comes.

In Closing

Thank you for joining us in this journey through level 2. EFT is a profoundly powerful tool for good in the world, and we are happy you have chosen to improve and refine your EFT skills. We encourage you to continue to explore your own Palace of Possibilities and to use all you have learned to help yourself and others.

References

Adams, A. (2001). Using EFT for Severely Emotionally Disturbed Children. In Craig, G. (Producer), *Specialty Series I* [DVD]. USA: Craig.

Adams, A. (2008). *Insider's Guide to Marketing Your EFT Practice.* [CD]. Media, PA: Vision Stream Studios.

Adams, A. (2009a). *In Pursuit of Excellence.* [DVD]. Media, PA: Vision Stream Studios.

Adams, A. (2009b). The pursuit of excellence. In P. Bruner & H. Bullough (eds.), *EFT and Beyond: Cutting Edge Techniques for Personal Transformation.* (pp. 41-67). Walden, UK: Energy Publications.

Adams, A. (2011a). *EFT4PowerPoint: Your Comprehensive Training Package.* [CD]. Rome, GA: self-produced.

Adams, A. (2011b). EFT4PowerPoint level 2 speaker's notes. *In EFT4PowerPoint: A Comprehensive EFT Training Package.* [CD] Rome, GA: self-produced.

Adams, A., & Davidson, K. (2011). *EFT Level 1 Comprehensive Training Resource.* Fulton, CA: Energy Psychology Press.

Altilio, T. (November–December 2007). Pain management: Speaking to social work. *Social Work Today* 7(6), 44.

American Psychiatric Association. (2000). *Diagnostic and Statistical Manual of Mental Disorders* (4th ed., text rev.). doi:10.1176/appi.books.9780890423349

Apkarian, A. V., Hashmi, J. A., & Baliki, M. N. (March 2011). Pain and the brain: Specificity and plasticity of the brain in clinical chronic pain. *Pain Amsterdam* 152(3)(Suppl.1), S49-S64. Retrieved from

http://www.sciencedirect.com/science/article/B6T0K-51PB8VB-2/2/948e897b2
e447a6ab021dea448e9a2df

Bromm, B., Desmedt, J. E., & Bodnar, R. J. (January 1997). Pain and the brain: From nociception to cognition. *Contemporary Psychology* 42(6), 514.

Bruner, P., & Bullough J. (eds.). (2009). *EFT and Beyond: Cutting Edge Techniques for Personal Transformation*. Walden, UK: Energy Publications.

Callahan, R. (1985). *Five Minute Phobia Cure*. Wilmington, DE: Enterprise Publishing.

Callahan, R. & Callahan, J. (1996). *Thought Field Therapy (TFT) and Trauma: Treatment and Theory*. La Quinta, CA: Self-published.

Carrington, P. (2006). *The Magic of Personal Choice in EFT: An Introduction to the EFT Choices Method*. Retrieved from http://www.newthoughtfamilies.com/Books/FreeEBooks/TheMagicofChoicesinEFT.pdf

Church, D., Geronilla, L., & Dinter, I. (January 2009) *International Journal of Healing and Caring* 9(1).

Cowley, M. (nd). *TFT Trauma Relief Technique*. Retrieved January 8, 2012, from http://tfttraumarelief.wordpress.com/instructions-for-tft-trauma-relief-technique/english/

Craig, G. (1999). The Tearless Trauma EFT technique. Retrieved from http://theamt.com/the_tearless_trauma_technique.htm

Craig, G. (2002). *Steps Toward Becoming the Ultimate Therapist: The Transcript*. Retrieved from http://www.scribd.com/doc/2532815/Tut-Trans

Craig, G. (2008a). *EFT for Back Pain: A Specialized Use of Emotional Freedom Techniques*. Retrieved from http://www.scribd.com/doc/49762158/EFT-for-back-pain

Craig, G. (2008b). Tutorial #4: Finding the core issue. *EFT Intermediate Library*. Retrieved from http://www.danachivers-eft.com/emofree/ExamInfo/Tutorials/FindingTheRightWords.pdf

Craig, G. (2008c). Tutorial #5: The anatomy of an emotional issue. *EFT Intermediate Library*. Retrieved from http://www.danachivers-eft.com/emofree/ExamInfo/Tutorials/AnatomyOfAnEmotionalIssue.pdf

Craig, G. (2008d). Tutorial #6: Customizing your Setup phrases. *EFT Intermediate Library*. Retrieved from http://www.danachivers-eft.com/emofree/ExamInfo/Tutorials/CustomizingTheSetup.pdf

Craig, G. (2008e). Tutorial #7: Reframes. *EFT Intermediate Library*. Retrieved from http://www.scribd.com/doc/19470262/EFT-Tutorial

Craig, G. (2008f). Tutorial #10: Conducting a Borrowing Benefits group. *EFT Intermediate Library*. Retrieved from http://www.danachivers-eft.com/emofree/ExamInfo/Tutorials/BBGroupSessions.pdf

Craig, G. (2009). The timeless EFT principles (And why EFT is always on the cutting edge). Retrieved from http://imcconsultingnigeria.com/docs/The%20Timeless%20EFT%20Principles.doc

Craig, G. (nda). *The Palace of Possibilities: Using EFT to Achieve One's Potential*. Retrieved from http://www.scribd.com/doc/2532816/Using-EFT-to-Achieve-Ones-Potential.

Craig, G. (ndb). Tutorial #7: Finding core issues. *The EFT Tutorial*. Retrieved from http://www.scribd.com/doc/19470262/EFT-Tutorial

Crooks, J. (2006). EFT Level II Course Handout. Unpublished handout. London: Author. www.BeaconTraining.co.uk.

Ellerton, R. (2004). Reframing. *Renewal Technologies*. Retrieved from http://www.renewal.ca/nlp20.htm

Feinstein, D., Eden, D, & Craig, G. (2005). *The Promise of Energy Psychology: Revolutionary Tools for Dramatic Personal Change*. New York: Tarcher/Penguin.

Feinstein, D., with Eden, D. (2011). *Ethics Handbook for Energy Healing Practitioners*. Fulton, CA: Energy Psychology Press.

Feinstein, D., & Krippner, S. (2008). *Personal Mythology: Discovering the Guiding Stories of your Past – Creating a Vision for your Future* (3rd ed.). Santa Rosa, CA: Elite Books.

Felitti, V., Anda, R., Nordenberg, D., et al. (1998) Relationship of childhood abuse and household dysfunction to many of the leading causes of death in adults: The Adverse Childhood Experiences (ACE) study. *American Journal of Preventive Medicine* 14:245–258.

Frank, A. (2011). www.JumpStartYourEFTPractice.com

Gallo, F. (2000). *Energy Diagnostic and Treatment Methods*. New York: WW Norton.

Gladwell, M. (2005). *Blink: The Power of Thinking Without Thinking*. New York: Little, Brown.

Hass, R. (2011). Reducing potential legal risks for practitioners: Do you have an alternative healing practice? What I discovered about how to reduce potential legal risks. Retrieved from http://www.intuitivementoring.com/reducing-legal-risks/

Hover-Kramer, D. (2011). *Creating Healing Relationships - Professional Standards for Energy Therapy Practitioners*. Santa Rosa, CA: Energy Psychology Press.

James, W. (1884). What is an emotion? *Mind* 9:188–205.

Karatzias, T., Power, K., Brown, K., McGoldrick, T., Begum, M., Young, J. Loughran, P., Chouliara, Z., & Adams, S. (2011) *The Journal of Nervous and Mental Disease* 199(6): 372-378.

Kenny, L. (2008). Change Your Mind with EFT (The Ultimate EFT Workbook – Level 2.) Unpublished handout. San Francisco, CA: Author www. lifecoachingwithlindsay.com

LaCombe, S. (December 23, 2008). Carl Rogers theory and his client centered approach. Retrieved from http://www.myshrink.com/counseling-theory.php?t_id=87

Levine, P. (1997). *Waking the Tiger: Healing Trauma*. Berkeley, CA: North Atlantic Books.

Lincoln, M. (1991). *Messages From The Body: Their Psychological Meaning*. Cool, CA: Talking Hearts.

Moss, G. (2007). *EFT Level 2 Manual*. Unpublished handout. UK: author.

Moss, G. (nda). Three step surrogate tapping for animals. Retrieved from http://www.emotional-health.co.uk/documents/Animals-GM.pdf

Moss, G. (ndb). Weeding your emotional garden with EFT. Retrieved from http://www.eftmastersworldwide.com/content/weeding-your-emotional-garden-with-eft/

National Association of Social Workers. (2008). *Code of ethics of the National Association of Social Workers*. NASW Delegate Assembly. Retrieved from http://www.socialworkers.org/pubs/code/code.asp

O'Neill, J. V. (September 2003). Lost productivity, psychosocial damage are costs. Pain: not only a health care problem, *NASW News* 48 (8).

Penrose, W. O., & Phi Delta Kappa, B. N. (1979). A primer on Piaget. *Fastback* 128. Pert, C. (1999) *Molecules of Emotion: The Science Behind Mind-Body Medicine.* New York: Simon & Schuster.

Rowe, J. (2005). The effects of EFT on long-term psychological symptoms. *Counseling and Clinical Psychology Journal*, 2(3):104.

ScienceDaily. (October 10, 2007). Stress contributes to range of chronic diseases, review shows. Science News. *ScienceDaily.* Retrieved from
http://www.sciencedaily.com

Siegel, D. J. (2010). *The Mindful Therapist.* New York: Norton.

Smith, B. (2007). Cognitive shifts that work. Retrieved from
http://www.eftmastersworldwide.com/content/cognitive-shifts-that-work

Smith, M., Jaffe-Gill, E., & Segal, J. (2010). Understanding stress: Signs, symptoms, causes, and effects. Retrieved from
http://helpguide.org/mental/stress_signs.htm

Swingle, P., Pulos, L., & Swingle, M. K. (2005). *Journal of Subtle Energies & Energy Medicine* 15: 75-86.

Wells, S., Polglase, K., Andrews, H. B., Carrington, P., & Baker, A. H. (2003). *Journal of Clinical Psychology*, 59(9): 943-966.

Appendix A

Worldwide EFT Training and EFT Level 2 Comprehensive Training Resource

The concepts taught in this coursebook cover the required curriculum for EFT trainings as follows:

EFT Level 2 Comprehensive Training Resource Coursebook	EFT Universe Level 2 Training Modules	AAMET Level 2 Required Concepts
Part 1 – The Foundation	Module 9	Brief review of AAMET Level 1
Chapter 1 – Points	Module 15	Additional tapping points, Floor to ceiling eye roll, Additional tapping techniques
Chapter 2 – Testing	Module 12	More on testing
Part 2 – The Dungeon		
Chapter 3 – Peace without Pain	Module 10	More on "chasing the pain" techniques, Introducing working with trauma
Chapter 4 – Leaving the Dungeon	Module 10	
Part 3 – Opening the Doors to the Palace		

Chapter 5 – Writing on the Walls	Module 11	Writing on the walls concept, Identifying limiting beliefs
Chapter 6 – Reading the Writing	Module 12	Finding core issues
Chapter 7 – Erasing the Writing	Module 11	Introduction to using Intuition
Chapter 8 – Composing New Writing	Module 11	Rapport and Calibration skills, Introduction to reframing
Chapter 9 – Blocked Doorways		
Chapter 10 – Trap Doors	Module 14	Tail enders concept, Further techniques to overcome Psychological Reversal, Introduction to using positive choices
Part 4 – Lowering the Drawbridge		
Chapter 11 – Weeding the Garden		Practitioner maintenance and the importance of continuing self-work
Chapter 12 – Leaving the Palace	Module 16	Basic safety for self & client, EFT practice Issues
Chapter 13 – Working with Special Populations	Module 13 Module 15 Module 16	EFT via the telephone / computer, Delivering EFT to groups and borrowing benefits
Chapter 14 – Continuing the Journey		

Appendix B

Working with Unconscious Dynamics: Uncovering Core Issues in Everyday Problems

by David Feinstein, PhD

The notion that the mind has multiple levels, including layers that are outside of awareness, can be found in Vedic texts written some 4,500 years ago. The concept that it is possible to systematically explore unconscious dynamics for therapeutic purposes was first articulated in the West by the Renaissance physician Paracelsus and studiously developed more than a century ago by Sigmund Freud and his followers. Contemporary scientists recognize that the vast majority of the brain's activities occur without the person's awareness and even the perceptions that drive our feelings may occur without being consciously registered.

We are all familiar with activities that do not reach the threshold of our awareness. Notice your next breath. You just brought an activity that would have most likely been outside your consciousness into your awareness. Many of the things we do, such as steering a car or walking to the refrigerator, can be done with little conscious attention. Likewise, our feelings, perceptions, thoughts, fears, desires, and motivations often operate outside our awareness. Bringing some of these into awareness can be a critical step not only in psychotherapy, but also in any endeavor intended to enhance psychological development and increase emotional freedom.

Three Ways EFT Addresses Unconscious Dynamics

Myriad innovative approaches for bringing unconscious dynamics into consciousness have been developed since Freud's day. Some are as simple as knowing where to look.

• Unrecognized internal objections to a conscious goal, called "psychological reversals" in EFT, can be identified by simple questioning that leads the mind to stumble upon such objections. "How would your life be different if you were no longer afraid to speak in public?" "Is it possible for someone who came from a broken family like yours to have a fulfilling relationship?" "Would you still be safe if you were no longer terrified of heights?" Psychological reversals can undermine emotional as well as physical healing.

• "Tail-enders" are another way the unconscious mind prevents EFT from leading to a desired outcome. In a tail-ender, the person's self-image or belief system tacks a statement onto the tail end of an affirmation suggesting that the affirmation is not possible or desirable. For instance, a tail-ender to the affirmation "I maintain balance and harmony between my career and my personal life" might be "...but if I don't give my career 100 percent, it will take a nosedive, and me with it." Like psychological reversals, tail-enders can be identified by fairly straightforward inquiries, such as "The thing about me that makes it impossible for me to reach this goal is ____" "If I did reach this goal, the consequences would be ____" "In order to reach this goal, I would have to ____" "What I really want, rather than just this goal, is ____" "Thinking about this goal reminds me of ____" "I would be more willing to reach this goal if first ____"

• A third way that EFT works with unconscious dynamics involves unrecognized "aspects" of the presenting problem. With psychological reversals and tail-enders, the person can often identify the internal conflict based on direct inquiry. This focuses the conscious mind on fairly routine questions whose answers it can access even though the person may never before have thought about the connections that are revealed. This is the territory that Freud called the "preconscious mind," the layer between the conscious mind and the unconscious mind. The unconscious mind is often shrouded in unresolved emotional conflict or trauma as well as preverbal primal urges. Unrecognized aspects of an issue that may be blocking progress in an EFT session often dwell in this deepest layer of the psyche and may require sophisticated excavation tools to bring them to the surface. Basic EFT procedures for identifying unconscious aspects of a problem when the SUD rating is not going down might include asking the person to focus on internal experiences and report:

• Any unusual emotion or bodily feeling.
• Any remembered sensation or emotion.
• Any image or remembered event.

This provides material that can then be elaborated (e.g., "Imagine that the sensation has a color and describe its color, shape, and size") or explored more fully (e.g., "Go back into the memory that just emerged and sense into what you were feeling in that situation").

While effective, these are gentle entries into the world of the unconscious mind.

Active Interventions into the Unconscious Mind

The shrouded nature of unconscious dynamics is, however, such that key elements of an issue may stay hidden without interventions that are highly focused and disciplined. The field of psychotherapy has developed many such approaches for delving into unconscious dynamics. Among those that trace back to Freud and his followers are:

- **Dream Work.** Freud called dreams "the royal road to the unconscious."
- **Analyzing Transference.** The therapeutic relationship provides a laboratory wherein the client's emotional reactions and psychological projections onto the therapist and the therapeutic process reveal deeper and deeper aspects of the person's unconscious dynamics.
- **Free Association.** The client puts into words whatever comes to mind, creating a kind of "focused spontaneity" that often allows deeper layers of the psyche to emerge.
- **"Freudian Slips."** Slips of the tongue and other ways that unconscious dynamics might reveal themselves in everyday life can be noticed and explored for their deeper meanings.
- **Hypnosis.** While eventually abandoned by Freud in favor of other methods, clinical hypnosis remains a powerful tool for working with unconscious dynamics.
- **Active Imagination.** In this technique, which was developed by Freud's colleague, Carl Jung, contents of the psyche are systematically translated into images, personified, and/or elaborated into stories.

Psychotherapists have since developed many other methods for exploring unconscious dynamics. Some of the more well known include psychodrama, breath work, guided imagery, Gestalt dialogue, voice dialogue, parts work, focusing, and the affect bridge.

Critical Issue. The fact that powerful methods exist for uncovering and working with unconscious dynamics does not mean that the EFT practitioner who is not trained as a psychotherapist should use them. To restate the EFT cautionary maxim: "Don't go where you don't belong!" Any psychological intervention used with an emotionally unstable person can lead to harmful and even disastrous results if the practitioner is not competent to field what occurs, such as abreactions, dissociation, regression, transference, and projective identification. If you do not know the meaning of these terms, you probably should not be offering EFT to the general public unless you have training that equips you to accurately identify individuals who are suffering from psychiatric disorders and are prepared to make appropriate referrals. This is true for any EFT practitioner who is not also a licensed mental health services provider, but it is particularly important before using aggressive procedures for uncovering unconscious dynamics.

Accessing Unconscious Material Without Aggressive Interventions

Assuming, however, that you are working with clients whose goals and emotional condition are within the scope of your training and credentialing, understanding the place of unconscious dynamics and appropriate ways of encountering them is critical to your success as a practitioner. It is, in fact, impossible *not* to engage unconscious dynamics in an effective EFT practice, even as a management consultant, life coach, or performance enhancement coach. Unconscious material comes into consciousness as part of an organic process as the more superficial layers of a problem are resolved. This occurs regularly enough that your work with a client will naturally deepen if you mindfully attend to whatever enters the client's awareness.

The use in EFT of the phrase "peeling away the layers of the onion" provides a visual metaphor of going deeper and deeper toward the core of a psychological issue without aggressive interventions. A physiological dimension of this natural unfolding of awareness is rooted in the hippocampus, the part of the brain that forms story-like memories out of our experiences. The hippocampus cannot integrate experiences when stress chemicals are being produced. That is the key to many dysfunctional emotional patterns.

Say your father was highly critical of your achievements. Each judgmental word, facial expression, and voice tone from a primary caregiver could have initiated a stress response that prevented your hippocampus from being able to adequately integrate the experiences into your understanding of yourself and your world. Instead, the experiences get stored in what is called "implicit memory" as dissociated, fragmented images of your father's words, look, and tone, with the original memory often unavailable. But following an achievement in your adult life, if anyone makes a comment that can possibly be interpreted as having a hint of criticism, those stored memory fragments are evoked to the extent that you are thrust into the emotional state you were in when your father criticized you as a child. You probably aren't recalling your father's criticisms at that moment, just feeling roundly judged, and the friend, colleague, or family member is wondering why you are overreacting to such an innocuous statement.

Suppose your friend commented on your latest artistic output by saying, "That's an interesting painting." Even though you know your friend meant well and displayed all the nonverbal signs of providing a compliment, you feel devastated because the words weren't "That's a great painting," plus you believe that the word "interesting" is what people say when they are being too polite to say how bad they think something is. You were scanning with a lens that was looking for criticism and interpreting all input as signs that it is coming your way. Your friend is taken aback that you feel devastated. At some level you also recognize that you have overreacted. You tap on it. Your subjective distress when you recall your friend's comment starts at a 9. You tap on the interchange, and after several rounds it is at a 5. Definite relief, but subsequent rounds won't bring it down any further. You are stuck. Later in the day, you have a vivid memory of your father coming to your first gymnastics performance and commenting with some disgust, even though you scored well, about flaws in your routine. You make the connection. The onion is unpeeling. You tap on that memory and get it down to a 2 when another memory appears in which your father screamed at you and punished you because you got a C on the math part of your second grade report card. You had come home so proud because you had A's in all the other subjects. By the time you have cleared a few memories like these, you return to your friend's comment about your painting. It is quickly down to a 0 and you are forever after less vulnerable to feeling devastated by similar comments that may come your way.

What has occurred in your brain is that the part of your limbic system or "emotional brain" that recognizes physical or emotional threat, specifically the "lateral nucleus" of the *amygdala*, has been scanning your interpersonal environment for criticism. It may find criticism even in innocent words, subtleties in tone of voice, or minute facial expressions. It does not matter that the person delivering the feedback was not meaning to be critical at all. The criticism-detection mechanism in the amygdala has become highly refined to the point of distortion. So the implicit memories of your father criticizing you are easily evoked, all this outside of your consciousness, and you are simply aware of feeling emotionally assaulted and then angry, depressed, or whatever secondary reactions you might go into.

By neutralizing, via tapping, the emotional impact of a series of memories that were formative in the emotional pattern, you are able to bring the memory to mind with no physiological distress. The hippocampus is then able to integrate the memory, and the physiological landscape of your brain literally changes. The pathways in the amygdala's lateral nucleus that initiated the stress response to the word "interesting" are erased or, in neurological terms, "depotentiated." Your thinking brain, the prefrontal cortex, can now also get into the act so you are able to reflect on dynamics that were outside the reach of your consciousness, gain new insights about them, and observe the way your self-concept shifts around the issue.

The SUD Rating as a Side Door into Mindful Awareness

Tapping that takes the emotional edge off of the issues that are initially presented allows deeper layers of an entrenched pattern to emerge and to be addressed with additional tapping. That is how EFT normally proceeds with anything but the most superficial of problems. But EFT, somewhat unintentionally, also utilizes a process that has been recently embraced by the psychotherapy field called "mindfulness" or mindful awareness.

Although mindfulness is among the most recent additions to the toolkits of contemporary clinicians, it is, interestingly, derived from one of the most ancient spiritual practices on the planet – meditation. Mindfulness, briefly, involves bringing your complete attention to your present experience on a moment-to-moment basis. Rather than acting on or judging your sensations, feelings, images, thoughts, or impulses, you simply notice them. Each sensation, feeling, image, thought, or impulse that arises during present-centered awareness is acknowledged and accepted as it is. This opens your field of awareness immensely.

Teaching clients how to give a SUD rating to their internal distress about a situation invites them into a state of mindfulness. "Notice any sensations, images, feelings, or thoughts as you imagine yourself back in the scene." Even after the person has given a 0 to 10 rating to the subjective distress in the scene, further mindful exploration can be invited. "How do you know it is a 5?" "What is the texture of the sensations you are reporting in your chest?" "When you recall the scene that just came to mind, what happens in your body?"

The process of establishing a SUD rating can evoke a deeply mindful state and be a powerful way of tuning into dynamics that had been outside the person's conscious awareness. Establishing a mindful attitude during EFT, and particularly during SUD ratings, is a gentle, non-invasive way of inviting unconscious dynamics to emerge.

Mindfulness as a Gentle Form of Inquiry

Just as questioning (e.g., "Describe the first time you can recall feeling this way") can be used for interpersonal inquiry into hidden aspects of an issue, mindfulness can also be used for internal inquiry. This can be done during or apart from taking a SUD rating. I recently came to a point where I was stuck on a personal issue, and my way through it illustrates the use of mindfulness with EFT. What emerged was an early experience that was driving a dysfunctional response pattern, though I had no idea how the two could be related.

My wife, Donna Eden, and I have, on occasion, been teaching a seminar called "The Energies of Love" since 1980, and our publisher wanted us to write a book on the topic. We know, however, of several couples that have written books on couple's work whose marriages dissolved shortly after their book was published and had become successful. Besides the embarrassment that would be involved, we did not want to tempt the relationship gods. We were wary about the arrogance of holding ourselves out as a couple who had "figured it out."

And sure enough, as soon as we were seriously discussing the book with our publisher, our relationship took a serious downhill turn. Our organization happened to be exploding at the time, growing exponentially. We were both under tremendous stress, and we weren't seeing eye-to-eye on many of the critical decisions we were making that would shape the future of our organization and our life's work. To make it worse, the energetic styles we relied on when under stress, one of the topics of our proposed book, seemed to be getting so exaggerated that is was hard to reach one another. Donna is highly expressive emotionally while I want to crawl into my emotional cave and regroup at times of distress. So she would feel unmet and discounted, and this would, of course, escalate her sense of distress. Realizing I could not escape, I tried to center myself for each hot topic we would encounter, but I began to respond in a way that I could hardly believe was me. Without the sanctuary of my cave, and with Donna being very animated about her opinions and upset, I would blow up. I would begin to scream at her, swear at her, and generally escalate a situation that was already too escalated.

After each incident, I would will myself to not get triggered the next time. I would tap. I could get it down to about a 3 or 4, and that perhaps helped a bit. I would then enter the next encounter centered, clear, and confident, but within five minutes, find myself screaming again and slamming doors. What an ominous atmosphere for writing our magnum opus on relationships! One day after it had happened for about the fifteenth time in three months, I went out to the hot tub of the condominium where we were staying. Fortunately, no one else was there.

I set my intention on noticing the texture of my experience at the time of these explosions and right before them. With that in place, I simply followed my breathing and noticed what emerged. At first was a lot of inner chatter, self-justifications, self-judgments, anger at Donna, seeing Donna's sweet countenance having turned fierce in hurt and frustration, fear of being discovered to be a fraud, images of the headline in our energy e-letter announcing the divorce of the self-proclaimed relationship virtuosos. I just noticed each and let it go. Back to the breath. Then a very vague image emerged. But I could place it. It was the bus stop where I was left off every day after school during first grade. Me and another boy were the only two left off there. Unfortunately for me, he was the class bully, a heavy set but very strong boy who went by the name of Pudgy. I remember that his father was a police officer and he was the toughest kid and the best fighter in our class. I, on the other hand, was tall, skinny, highly uncoordinated, painfully shy, and socially awkward – the perfect target for bullies of far less stature than Pudgy. So it wasn't a big rush for him to beat me up, and I usually got away with just a punch to the stomach or jaw, just enough to make me cry. Once he was satisfied that he had done enough damage to reaffirm his bully status, he would turn away and walk home.

But on the day that came up in my vision, something unusual had happened in school. The teacher was mad at the class for being unruly. We didn't get recess. But she had to deal with us needing a bathroom break, so she had all the boys line up in one line, all the girls in another, and marched us to the boys' and girls' lavatories. But first she gave a warning that if even one of us spoke, the entire class would have to put their heads down for thirty minutes afterward, a most unwelcome punishment for children with growing, restless bodies. If we retained perfect silence during the bathroom break, she would instead read us a story we were all eager to hear. After I finished at the urinal, I walked up to the sink to wash my hands and another boy walked up to it at the same time. I stepped back and invited him to go first. At that unfortunate moment, the teacher happened to look into the boys' bathroom, saw me talking, and that was that. The whole class spent the next half hour with our collective heads on our folded arms on our little desks. The teacher did not announce the name of the culprit, but she said it was someone she never would have suspected. Of course, by the end of the school day, everyone knew it was me. I could not have been more humiliated or felt more ostracized.

It also gave occasion for Pudgy to give me an extra-vigorous beating that day. And that was the scene that emerged out of the initial vague image of the bus stop. I was surprised it came up right then, in part because I had decades earlier dealt with my relationship with Pudgy ad nauseam in psychodynamic talk therapy. I felt done with it, processed, complete. I particularly didn't, at first, see any relationship between this memory and my arguments with Donna. But even as I kept bringing my awareness back to my breath, I had opened a portal that kept presenting different aspects of the memory and then connections to my current problem. While no one would ever see Donna as a bully, as we got out of harmony with the pressures on us, the complex demands of the organization, and the curse of having agreed to hold our relationship up as a model, we became about as acrimonious as we'd ever been in our thirty-three years together. I felt I was giving my heart and soul to the organization and Donna's disagreement and judgment of my best efforts felt as unfair as becoming the class villain for having simply told another boy he could use the sink first. The sense of unfairness and injustice was the invisible link between what I was playing out with Donna and what was still unhealed in my psyche. By tapping on that, it lost its power, and my reactions to more recent altercations could be neutralized as well. I've not been hooked in one of those discussions since. This had a domino effect. Now Donna could express her frustrations and be heard rather than fought, allowing genuine problem-solving to occur, and we were soon back on track with one another.

I was on my own in that situation. We were living outside the country at the time and did not have ongoing access to a therapist we trusted or to our most resourceful friends. I was desperate, as each unresolved encounter was not only damaging our relationship, but the unsolved problems were also hurting our organization in ways that were making our lives more difficult. I have a large bag of clinical tricks, but mindfulness was the one that popped me through the doorway. The sense of feeling bullied wasn't even registering in my consciousness while the pattern was in play. I would simply be in a discussion with Donna about a sensitive issue and suddenly and uncharacteristically find myself screaming at her. Work with unconscious dynamics was the only route that was going to change the pattern. Of the myriad images, feelings, sensations, and thoughts that emerged while I was inwardly attuned, the vague image of the bus stop was accompanied by a sense of it being important enough to explore further, and it turned out to be the gold nugget in the stream-of-consciousness grains of sand.

Establishing the SUD rating when progress is slower than expected is a natural opportunity to teach the client mindfulness. But there is a twist in the way it works during an EFT session. Rather than the inquiry being a totally solitary and internal process, it becomes part of a dialogue with the practitioner. I, as the practitioner, also keep myself in a mindful state, yet the space is opened to the client's words and nonverbal communication as well as to my own internal world. I have found that it is easier for clients who are not practiced in mindfulness (so this can be done in the opening session) to track their internal experiences when the exploration is part of a back-and-forth interchange with the practitioner. In the process, I can become exquisitely attuned to the client's internal world. And mindfulness uncovers not only buried trauma and repressed conflicts, but it also allows our deepest intuitive wisdom to come into awareness.

Systems for Working with Unconscious Dynamics

More than thirty different approaches to energy psychology are being practiced, with EFT being just one of them. Many of these are distinguished by having
their own models and procedures for addressing the unconscious dynamics that
are involved in a client's difficulties, unrealized potentials, or next developmental
step. It is not possible in the space of this article to try, even briefly, to summarize
the various approaches, but I will give an example of how tapping can be combined with other approaches for pursuing deep psychological work.

My first job as a psychologist was to serve as an instructor in psychiatry in
the School of Medicine at Johns Hopkins. While there, I conducted an investiga-
tion of forty-six of the more than two hundred "new therapies" that had emerged
by the early 1970s. From this, I culled what I considered the best techniques into
a program for helping people actively and mindfully involve themselves in fur-
thering their psychological and spiritual development. The focus of this program
was on the evolving personal myths – the guiding but often unconscious schemas
– that shape our lives. Since much of this process is outside our awareness (the
great scholar of mythology Joseph Campbell said that once an early culture could
name one of its myths, that myth was already dead), the program I developed
focused a great deal on unconscious dynamics.

As is now recognized by psychologists as well as neurologists, consciousness
expands as a process of "differentiation" and "integration" (see, for instance, Dan
Siegel's *The Mindful Therapist*). In the terms I was developing, a guiding myth
becomes outmoded as the individual matures and the psyche generates what I
called a "counter-myth" that challenges it. In the personal mythology program,
I taught people to *differentiate* between the old myth and the counter-myth – to
explore them until each was well articulated and well understood. It then became
possible to *integrate* them into a new, larger, more-attuned guiding image that
would better serve the person's current circumstances and level of development.
I identified a five-stage process by which this occurred naturally, along with a
corresponding five-stage model for facilitating a more harmonious, effective, and
mythically-attuned way of advancing a person's consciousness.

I continued to develop this model, working with the renowned consciousness researcher, psychologist Stanley Krippner, over the next three decades,
with the most recent addition being the introduction of tapping during each of
the five stages:

• The first stage of mythic transformation involves the breakdown of a guiding myth. This is often a painful process and it can also be painful to fully explore
the territory. Unresolved or traumatic memories often emerge. I found that by
tapping on the pain and trauma as it appeared, it became possible for people to
navigate their way through this stage more quickly and with much less distress.

• The second stage of the process attends to the developing counter-myth.
The program helps people cultivate receptiveness to deep intuitive insight during this stage. Psychological reversals are almost always involved with mythic
change, and they can be addressed by stimulating energy points while articulat-

ing Setup Statements such as, "Even though I feel trapped in my old mythology, I choose to open myself to fresh insight and direction."

• In the third stage of the work, the old myth and the counter-myth confront one another in a natural struggle for dominance. Facilitating a resolution can avoid much pain and misguided effort in the person's life. Tapping can be used to help the person accept and become creative about mythic turmoil he or she does not know how to resolve. The new direction may seem appealing but unreachable. The old, dysfunctional myth is familiar and may still bring comfort. A statement for accepting the conflict while moving toward its resolution might be, "Even though I can't see the resolution of this conflict, I choose to know that forces deep in my psyche are already mobilizing toward a new and creative solution."

• Additional stages of the work might use tapping to reduce tail-enders as a new myth is articulated, to confront self-judgment when progress is slower than wished, to counter the impulse to act according to the old myth, and to affirm the new mythic direction.

Unconscious dynamics may be uncovered organically or through focused effort. EFT uses many gentle methods that tend to spontaneously reveal the psychic forces that underlie a client's presenting problems. As these come into view, new understandings of the client's difficulties emerge, new ways to approach them become apparent, and triggers that were evoking a stress response may quickly be declawed. The personal mythology model illustrates that tapping can also be integrated with other approaches for more systematically delving deeply into the psyche. Few terrains are more interesting.

David Feinstein, PhD, is a clinical psychologist who has served on the faculties of the Johns Hopkins University School of Medicine and Antioch College. Author of eight books and more than eighty professional articles, he has been a pioneer in the areas of energy psychology and energy medicine. His books have won eight national awards, including the *U.S. Book News* Best Psychology/Mental Health Book in 2007 (for *Personal Mythology*) and an *Indies* Best Books Award (for *The Promise of Energy Psychology*). His website is www.EnergyPsychEd.com.

Appendix C

Teaching EFT to Kids

Handout from Ann Adam's presentation in Gary Craig's *Specialty Series I*

Steps for Getting Started

- **"The first step is to think about your problem."** If the child is already upset, you can skip this step since it's obvious the child is thinking about or feeling something about the issue. However, explaining this step is important in teaching this exercise to children so that they understand they *have to "tune in" to the particular issue* they want to work on. Explain that "This exercise will calm you down and help you think more clearly about your problem. If you learn this exercise, you can be upset only when *you* choose to be upset."

- **"Now we want to know how upset you are."** For younger children, have them use out-stretched arms to measure show how upset the they are. Use hands in a prayer position indicating no upset. With some children you can put your own arms out to measure and let the child nod when you reach the right amount of upset. Older children have no problem with telling you on a 0 to 10 scale how upset they are, but even some of the older children respond well to your outstretched arms for measurement. It seems to help them "get into it" better with your participation.

- **"OK, the first step is to tap the side of your hand."** Show them by using your own hand as an example how to tap on the fatty side of the hand. Be sure to tap the side of the hand rather than banging the hand on something. You can tell the child it is called the Karate Chop spot. This spot can also be introduced as the "friendly spot" since that's where you touch another person's hand when you shake hands to show you are "friendly." Make a Setup statement such as **"Even though I have this problem, I am a super kid,"** or, **"I am a good person"** or, **"I deeply and completely accept myself,"** etc. It doesn't seem to matter whether the child says the words or you say the words for the child. If a child has a particularly bad self image use a slight variation such as "I want to accept myself."

Some kids say that tapping the karate spot is calming all by itself. Use your judgment in choosing to use Setup statements; it depends on the kid and/or the situation. Setup statements are a great help in getting in touch with what is really going on, but are not absolutely necessary to significantly calm the child. Suspicious or oppositional children are rarely willing to use the Setups.

EFT Short Cut:

- **First tapping point.** Use three or four fingers and tap between the eyebrows. (Tap about seven times.)
- **Second point.** Use two fingers of both hands and tap on the bony part under both eyes. (Tap about seven times.)
- **Third point.** Use a closed fist to the chest just below and to the left of the throat for the collarbone spot. (About seven times.) Can cross arms and tap both sides.
- **Fourth point.** Tap under both arms. This is like giving a yourself a hug. Wrap arms around your body and pat under both arms about a palm's width below the armpit. For younger children you can call this the "monkey spot" and have them tap with each hand under the same arm. They get a kick out of this! (Tap about seven times.)
- **Repeat this exercise three times for a particular problem or until the upset goes away.** Sometimes when one problem is calmed, another related problem comes up, and the child must repeat the process for the second problem.

The above exercise using the short cut is very effective (80% +) for anxiety or upsetting situations.

Many texts on acupuncture suggest that the meridians are tied to particular organs and emotions. John Diamond, an Australian psychiatrist, developed this idea into the Acupuncture Emotional System (AES) and it's widely used. Whether the idea will eventually be proven scientifically, or not, it is useful in holistic practice, and kids really seem to like relating a point to a feeling or a part of the body. Incorporating this idea into EFT sometimes stimulates additional interest in the process for some children. According to Diamond, tapping the side of hand can mitigate sadness and release joy, the point inside the eyebrow can relieve frustration and bring calm. More on Diamond's ideas can be found in his book, *Life Energy: Using the Meridians to Unlock the Hidden Power of the Emotions*.

In doing this exercise with children, use varying language and keep it fun and light-hearted. Repetitive rounds of EFT get boring for some children. Add in the finger points for variety after the child is calmer but when more work needs to be done. Also, use the 9 gamut to vary the exercise. Tap, using all of the EFT points. Use the "sore spot" instead of the gamut spot. Tap the thymus with all five fingers. Some children prefer to TAB – Touch and Breathe. Varying how you do the exercise keeps it interesting. When teaching children, having them write the steps down or draw a picture of them can increase their "ownership" of the process. Let them name the process themselves.

• If the child feels bad about what happened or feels responsible or guilty, tell the child to **"Tap on the body side of the fingernail on the index finger."** Tell the child **"This is the 'guilty' finger. Tapping it helps to make the bad feeling inside go away."** If the child is willing, try adding the forgiveness exercise. While tapping on the index finger have them say three times **"I forgive myself; I was doing the best I could."**

• If the child is angry about what happened tell the child **"Tap on the body side of the fingernail on the little finger. This is the 'angry' finger. Tapping it helps make the angry feelings go away."** If the child is willing, continue the forgiveness exercise, have them say three times while tapping: **"I forgive my 'friend/mother/father/ teacher/staff/etc.' They were doing the best they could."** If the child won't buy that or is not ready just have them say **"I forgive…; they were just being a 'jerk' and that's what jerks do."**

• **Explain to the child that EFT can be used any time he/she is upset about anything.** The exercise helps the child calm down quickly so that he/she can think more clearly about solutions to the situation. It is sometimes amazing to watch the solutions that come to the child after a round of tapping or TAB. Help the child problem solve and plan what to do next to resolve the problem. Encourage the child to teach others. Have him/her practice teaching you.

• **Tap or TAB along with the child.** It calms you down, too! Use EFT for any of your own upsets. Try tapping on the way home from work about the aggravations of your day. You will be calm, ready to meet the issues at home, and be more emotionally available to your family. And don't forget to tap for any aggravation the child may cause you!

• Complex problems involving many layers of trauma or behaviors, such as temper tantrums, require much repetition. Make the process part of the daily routine. Use for "tucking in" at night. Use after school for concerns of the day that may reflect earlier traumas. Use in the morning if a child is nervous about any activity of the day. Use any, and every time, the child starts to become upset.

Remember:

- Identify the problem to work on.
- Tune in to the feeling or problem.
- Identify any new aspects.
- Use it for everything and be creative in your approaches.
- Persistence counts. Keep at it.
- Make it a routine part of every day.

Ideas for Introducing EFT to Emotionally Disturbed Children

Handout from Ann Adam's presentation in Gary Craig's *Specialty Series I*

Remember to

- Treat each child with respect and dignity.
- Let them sense your admiration for their courage in "keepin' on keepin' on" in the face of, at times, unbelievable adversity. These children are truly doing the best they can.
- Totally focus on the individual child. Total focus really draws these children. They are unusually sensitive to inattentiveness. They have known lots of rejection and are generally hungry for the total attention of another person.
- Establish rapport. Rapport is about having the child feel comfortable with you. Rapport is not about having a relationship or trust – those take time. Rapport is about having the child feel that, in some way you, are "like" him or her. Sometimes, establishing rapport is as simple and as quick as matching the child's facial expression or body position.
- Take a playful approach. Get creative; think outside the box.
- Let your clinical judgment guide you in what to say. Use the "get yourself out of the way" concept. Congruency is critical. What you say and do and feel must match.
- Always tap with the child. Keep tapping as they talk.
- Never touch the child without his or her permission.
- Make EFT "theirs." When possible have them write down the steps on a card or notebook. If the child doesn't write, draw pictures with/for him/her. Tie EFT to something familiar (i.e. other ways they relax and get comfort.)
- Answer their questions about the process honestly. They don't usually ask, but, when they do, only give as much information as they ask for and can understand given their developmental level.
- Take care of yourself.

Phraseology is infinite. Some suggestions:

- I know a way to calm you down quickly.
- This is a way to calm you down so you can think more clearly about your problem.
- I know something that is a little weird that could help your feelings. You look like you can handle weird. Want to try it?
- I know a trick to get over being mad – like that (snap fingers)
- I know this cool way to stop being upset in a hurry.

- I know a way that can fix being upset very quickly. It's kinda different. I bet you never saw it before.
- I can see you are really worried about this; want to try something tha could make you less worried?
- Ya know, I have this really great way to stop being upset. I usually use it with adults, but sometimes I teach it to kids too. I guess you are old enough.
- I have this really great way to stop being upset. Are you game to try it; it is sort of strange? Can you handle strange?
- I know a new relaxation exercise that works quickly most all the time. It doesn't take very long to do. Want to try it for that problem?
- This is a new exercise that came out of California. Kind of slow in getting to this area. You'd be one of the first to try it.
- Looks like you are all out of energy. If you tap right here we could see if we can bring back your energy.
- I have this little relaxation exercise you can use.
- You don't have to tell me what is bothering you. I have a way you can get over it and not even tell me what it was. You are totally in control and don't have to say anything.
- You can chose to be upset only when YOU want to be upset. I want to teach you something that you can use anytime YOU want to stop being upset.

"Even though..." set-up statements are simple: Use their words.

If you have a VERY good idea of what else may be going on, add your guess (and it is a guess), to the second or third time. But you can't go wrong using just what they tell you. Vary the wording of: I deeply and completely accept myself.

Some other ideas:

- There is a good person in me.
- I am a super kid.
- I'm a really good kid.
- I want to love and accept myself.
- I am a marvelous person.
- I am wonderful.
- I am generous and kind.
- I like myself.
- God loves me. Mother/father/etc. loves me (when they do).

Appendix D

How Science Evaluates EFT

by Dawson Church, PhD, CEHP,
best-selling author of *The Genie in Your Genes*

Why is research so vital to the widespread adoption of EFT? There are thousands of stories on the Internet written by people who have recovered from a wide variety of physical and psychological challenges using EFT. Although such anecdotal evidence is valuable in pointing to what EFT can do, rigorous scientific research has been required in order to establish EFT as an "evidence-based" method that can be used with confidence by medical and psychological professionals in primary care. That requires clinical trials published in peer-reviewed professional journals.

Empirically Validated Treatments

EFT researchers generally support the evidence-based standards defined by the American Psychological Association (APA) Division 12 (Clinical Psychology) Task Force ("APA standards," for short). This Task Force was set up in the early 1990s to produce a clear definition of an evidence-based practice. After a great deal of work, the Task Force defined an "empirically validated treatment" as one for which there are two different controlled trials conducted by independent research teams. For a treatment to be designated as "efficacious," the studies must demonstrate that the treatment is better than a wait list, placebo, or established efficacious treatment. To be designated as "probably efficacious," a treatment must have been shown to be better than a wait list in two studies that meet these criteria or are conducted by the same research team rather than two independent teams.

Statistical Significance

The APA standards advocate that studies contain sufficient subjects to achieve a level of statistical significance of $p < .05$ or greater, which means that there is only one possibility in 20 that the results are due to chance.

When researchers speak of the "size" of a study, they may not mean *how many participants* the study contained, but instead the *size of the statistical significance* obtained. The size of the significance is far more important in research than the number of subjects. (The APA Task Force report found the average number of subjects in each group in behavioral studies to be only 12.) When a treatment has *big* effects, it can be demonstrated with just a *few* subjects; a *weak* treatment requires a *great many subjects* to achieve statistical significance at the $p < .05$ level.

You can picture this by imagining two studies of cars. The first asks the research question, "How many times does a wheel have to rotate against the road in order to wear down the tires by a centimeter?" This requires many thousands of rotations (subjects) to give a $p < .05$ effect size, because each rotation has only a tiny effect. Compare it to another study, which asks the question, "Does removing a car's battery make it hard to start?" You only need to do this with a very few cars (subjects) to get a statistically significant $p < .05$, because removing the battery has a huge effect. A bigger effect shows up as a smaller p value; a study with $p < .0001$ means that there is only one possibility in 1,000 that the results are due to chance.

All the published studies of EFT have effects at the $p < .05$ level or better. EFT has met the APA standards as an "efficacious" or "probably efficacious" treatment for phobias, anxiety, depression, and posttraumatic stress disorder (PTSD).

In the field of medicine (as distinguished from the field of psychology), there are several definitions of what constitutes an "evidence-based" treatment. One of the most useful comes from the National Registry of Evidence-based Programs and Practices (NREPP) in the United States. It requires a standardized description of the method in the form of a manual and training materials, documentation that the treatment was delivered with fidelity to that method, the use of validated and reliable outcome measures, corrections for dropouts (such as an intent-to-treat analysis), appropriate statistical analysis, sample sizes sufficient to produce a probability of $p < .05$ or better, and publication in a peer-reviewed professional journal.

The State of EFT Research

While many important EFT research questions remain to be answered, a great deal of groundwork is already in place: EFT has been researched in more than seven countries, by more than sixty investigators, whose results have been published in more than fifteen different peer-reviewed journals. These include distinguished top-tier journals such as: the *Journal of Clinical Psychology;* the APA journals *Psychotherapy: Theory, Research, Practice, Training* and *Review of General Psychology;* and the oldest psychiatric journal in the United States, the *Journal of Nervous and Mental Disease.* EFT research has been conducted by investigators affiliated with many different institutions. In the United States, these range from Harvard Medical School to the University of California at Berkeley, to City University of New York, to Walter Reed Army Medical Center (USUHS), to Texas A&M University. Institutions in other countries whose faculty have contributed to EFT research include Lund University (Sweden), Ankara University (Turkey),

Santo Tomas University (Philippines), Lister Hospital (England), Cesar Vallejo University (Peru), and Griffith University (Australia). The wide variety of institutions, peer-reviewed journals, investigators, and settings that have, in independent research, found EFT to be efficacious are one indication of the breadth of existing research results. The next frontier of EFT research is replication of the studies that have not yet been replicated and investigations into the physiological changes that occur during EFT, using such tools as DNA microarrays (gene chips), MEG (magneto-encephalography), fMRI (functional magnetic resonance imaging), and neurotransmitter and hormone assays.

Types of Reports: Outcome Studies, Clinical Reports, Mechanisms Research, and Review Articles

There are several kinds of scientific papers. The most important, from the standpoint of those suffering from physical or psychological problems, is "outcome" research. This type of study compares the medical or psychological outcomes of two groups of people with similar symptoms, or the same people before and after treatment. Outcome studies measure changes in, for instance, pain, depression, or PTSD symptoms.

Whereas an outcome study is designed to answer the research question "Does this work?" the second kind of paper asks the question "How does it work?" With EFT having been shown in many outcome studies to work very quickly and reliably for a variety of ailments, researchers have become increasingly interested in the *physiological mechanisms of action* by which such rapid healing is possible. So the second kind of scientific paper is a mechanisms paper. An example of a mechanisms paper is a study that used EEG (electroencephalogram) machines to examine the brain waves of subjects before and after EFT. A important mechanisms paper studied the levels of cortisol, a major stress hormone. It compared the cortisol levels of people after EFT, talk therapy, and rest. It found that cortisol dropped much more in the EFT group.

A third category of paper is the "clinical report." Rather than using validated numerical instruments to assess outcomes, clinical reports describe the use of EFT with special groups, such as people with epilepsy, veterans, children, or prisoners. They may present a single case. Finally, there are "review papers." These gather together all the published evidence about a topic, present it in a structured manner, and evaluate that body of knowledge. You will find links to all these different types of paper under "Research" at EFTUniverse.com, which maintains a current bibliography of all EFT research.

If you're presenting EFT to a supervisor, hospital administrator, or medical professional, it's a great help to be able to print out a list of studies. This shows that EFT is backed up by credible scientific research, and that it's an "evidence-based" method.

Appendix E

Test Your Knowledge Answer Key

PAGE 49

"In order to work effectively with a client's issue, you need to know the specific details of the issue." is false.

All of the following statements are true of The Tearless Trauma Technique *except*
c. By definition, the technique is always tearless.

"When a client complains of a physical issue, you should recommend that a physician be consulted." is true.

"When pain doesn't decrease and just moves to a different location in the body, EFT is not working." is false.

Which technique begins with guessing what the intensity *would* be *if* the issue were to be the focus?
a. Tearless Trauma

Which option *best* defines Sneaking up?
a. Sneaking up addresses their fear without dealing with it directly.

When using the Tearless Trauma Technique you tap before you go directly to the event until the intensity is guessed to be
c. 3 – 0

"When emotional intensity is high, the client is ready for a breakthrough, so it's important to push on to resolution." is false.

PAGE 56

"The first step when using the Movie Technique is to instruct clients to run through the entire movie in their minds." is false.

All of the following are *true* of the Movie Technique *except:*
b. The movie should always be 3 minutes or less.

"The Tell the Story Technique can be used effectively along with the Watch the Movie Technique, or by itself." is true.

"When using the Tell the Story Technique, the client only has to tell the story once." is false.

PAGE 63

"All of the "writing on our walls" is negative and limiting." is false.

"We most often try to find a way to fit new experiences in to the "truth" that we already know." is true.

"The "writing on our walls" can be the result of something said to us, implied, or overheard." is true.

"Practitioners need to be aware of the "writing" on their own walls unless they are using gentle techniques where they don't need to know the details of their clients' issues." is false.

All of the below are true, *except*
d. We cannot change the learning of our past; we need just to get over it.

PAGE 72

"Often, you will work on several minor issues or events before finding the core issue." is true.

Which of the following statements is *true*?
d. None of the above.

"You should help the client dismiss irrelevant details that come up so that you can continue looking for the core issue." is false.

PAGE 85

"The specific language used for the acceptance part of the Setup is less important than assuring that whatever is said is a statement of acceptance that feels comfortable for the client." is true.

Which of the following is **not** an important step to address **before** starting a tapping sequence?
b. Recap the last EFT session.

"After tapping, if a client reports a 0 in intensity, it is okay to take her word for it." is false.

"When using the Setup and Reminder Phrase combination, you can modify your words based on the verbal and nonverbal cues of the client." is true.

"The only difference in the Extended Setup and the Setup/Reminder Combination is that one uses the Basic Recipe and the other uses the Full Basic Recipe." is false.

PAGE 93

"In EFT, a reframe is any statement that presents a new way of looking at an issue, and when used skillfully, can encourage a cognitive shift." is true.

"When our emotional reactions to events are neutralized, what happens *naturally* is a cognitive shift." is true.

Which of the following is *not* true?
d. Rapport is not a factor in reframes.

"Craig recommends you have solid EFT experience using standard EFT alone to collapse events and issues before beginning to use reframes." is true.

PAGE 100

All of the following are *true* of PTSD *except*
a. PTSD is caused by personally experiencing a life-threatening event.

"A person with PTSD can suffer from panic attacks, depression, substance abuse, and obsessive-compulsive behaviors." is true.

PAGE 105

"When dealing with phobias deal with any high intensity around the fear before getting specific details about the phobia" is true.

All of the following are good examples of a phobia, *except*
c. On a mountain hike, Sue nearly steps on a rattlesnake. She experiences instant near-panic symptoms, gasping for breath, shaking, and, ultimately, running away.

"It is a good idea to test the client's level of phobic response in vivo before beginning to tap on the overall issue and its many aspects." is false.

PAGE 109

"The sensation of pain moving around in the body is a common physiological response." is true.

All of the following statements are true, *except*
d. It's okay to tell people that EFT cures physical issues.

"Metaphor is useful in dealing with physiological reactions." is true.

PAGE 121

"It is important to consistently bring up the positive while tapping with a client because the client will begin to attract the desired results." is false.

An example of a tail-ender for the positive goal "I will get to work on time every day by setting my alarm clock for twenty minutes earlier" is
a. "But I've said that before and it never works."

"One way of addressing reversals is to recognize and appreciate the intent of the resistance." is true.

Which of the following often underlie negative beliefs?
e. All of the above

"One effective way to test for remaining tail-enders is to try to imagine a positive future without the tail-ender." is true.

PAGE 131

"If you are working on your own issues and get stuck, it is safe to assume there is a reversal or self-sabotage, and to look for the origin of the resistance." is true.

All of the following are true, *except:*
d. It is important to learn to address your own issues, and tapping along with other aids or sessions will only hinder your ability to work effectively for yourself.

PAGE 147

"It is important to consider both the positive and negative elements of using EFT over the phone before accepting a phone client." is true.

When working on the phone:
c. You need to pay closer attention to things like verbal clues, changes in vocal levels, and even your own intuition.

PAGE 149

"When Borrowing Benefits, as long as the observers tap along, it's not important that they tap on the same issue as the person they are watching." is true.

When demonstrating Borrowing Benefits, the presenter should do all except:
a. Conduct the best session possible for the volunteer, calling on any needed EFT tools.

PAGE 154

"When tapping for an animal or working with a surrogate, it is important to first clear your own issues around the event or situation." is true.

The following is a good example of making EFT accessible to children:
d. All of the above

"When working with children, it's important to first work on your own responses to the child's situaion in order to more effectively help the child work through his or her own emotions." is true.

CPSIA information can be obtained
at www.ICGtesting.com
Printed in the USA
BVOW11s1549161217
502766BV00003B/5/P